Resilient

IbbiLane Press

Copyright ©2016

ISBN-13: 978-0692694398 (IbbiLane Press)

ISBN-10: 0692694390

Lovingly and courageously dedicated to everyone who has ever endured domestic violence in their life. May these stories bring hope and healing and give you the strength to share your own story so that others may find hope and healing too.

Table of Contents

Marian Stenseth Evans	7
Wade Bloodgood	37
Sharon Gulley	65
Courtney Killian	79
Abigail Hope	85
Kim's Journey	101
Eden Wallace	161
Lisa James	173
Mary Kay Elsner	183
Kellie Fitzgerald	191

About the Author

This is a book on overcoming adversity and abuse. Enjoying the lessons and the blessings life has taught me. I found the joy of my own spirit and authentic self with a little help from my family and friends.

ACKNOWLEDGMENTS

First order of gratitude goes to those who believed in me and encouraged me to write. Thank You, Leisa Evans, Jody Doty, Kellie Fitzgerald and Alana Gorski, Brenda Fecht and my family Susan, Amanda and Dustin Griffith.

My Story: Marian (Stenseth) Evans

I was born by C-section in Sedro Woolley WA in 1945; my parents were farmers in Day Creek thirteen miles outside Sedro Woolley. It was a 120 acre chicken farm. They had 6,000 laying chickens and were part of the Co-Op. When I was a baby my Mom put me in a clothes basket and we spent the day in the chicken coop with her cleaning the eggs for market. She loved music so I grew up from the womb listing to music.

When I was about three years old the chicken coop burnt and only 2,000 chickens were left so they went into milking cows, haying and corn fields. I had a sister seven years older than me I was a surprise to the family. In Day Creek I had aunts, uncles and cousins and animals as friends. Day Creek had one General Store, one Church, the Grange Hall and a one room School House. Miss Clark was our teacher for first, second and third grade. This was at the end of

World War II and my uncles and cousins were coming home from the war. My parents had rations on gas, flour, sugar, coffee all kinds of things because they were farmers they got a few more rations. I remember my seven years on the farm fondly but as I got older I remembered my mother running through the woods with me tucked under her arm and having my sister run as fast as she could trying to get away from my father because he was beating her. She always ran to my Aunt Kathryn's and Uncle Ed's. My father was an alcoholic and terrorized my mother I never saw my father sober one day of my life he was already an alcoholic when I was born. My father never validated me or never saw me much. The rumor was he was not my father and that's how he always treated me as the red headed step child. I was unwelcome expect for my mother. I do remember being shy as a child so I wouldn't get in trouble.

In 1952 my parents sold the farm and moved into town Sedro Woolley, WA. My mom didn't know anyone in town and the beatings to her got worse. My sister was fourteen when she married. Her husband was also abusive to her and my mother. In 1953 my parents divorced and my father talked my mom into signing herself into Northern State Hospital. She was having a nervous breakdown and going through menopause. My father had already found another woman in Anacortes, WA and so he left me home alone for three months where no one came home. I was seven and a half. I made sure I was at school on time, changed into my play clothes as soon as I got home. I was afraid of what would happen to me if anyone knew I was abandoned.

I still have infinity for dogs, because that is how I survived is the neighbor's dogs shared their dinner scrapes with me. It was before the packaged dog food so I would go play after school with school friends after I watched the Mickey Mouse Club and see what their mom was cooking for dinner. In those days everyone had a dinner time and everyone ate at the table together and any unfinished food was given to the dogs. The dogs let me pick first so I survived. I was a contributor in Under the Red Roof, One Hundred Years at Northern State Hospital by M. J. McGoffin in 2011 about my experience of visiting my mother when she was in Northern State Hospital. I was all alone when school let out for the summer; I signed up for bible class and earned my first bible which I still have today. They say the first seven years is when a child is formed and my mother taught me to not only survive but enjoy the ride. Learn courage and how to be strong and independent with no one to guide you. I had to have a backbone not a wishbone there was no other choice.

After three months my aunt in Monroe, WA had reported to the CPS that she thought I was a child left home alone and that she wouldn't put it past my father. December 31, 1954 my father married my first step-mother and I was moved to Anacortes where my step-mother and step-bother lived.

I wasn't allowed in the house except to change my clothes after school, do chores and then I had to go outside and wait until my father came home. For a couple of years I slept on the couch until a small bedroom was added for me. My father was still drinking and an alcoholic and paid no attention to me. On a Sunday drive I asked if I was adopted and was told no. He did not physically abuse my step-mother like he did my mom but she would tell me how he sexually abused her which I didn't understand at the time. I was in fourth grade. I lived there from fourth grade to part of seventh grade. My step-brother molested me I was ten and he was fifteen when my father and Step-mother were at an evening church function. He couldn't penetrate me so he stuck it down my mouth. When they got home from church I was in my room crying all night and in the morning my father pulled me out of bed and they started drilling me. I wouldn't tell so they got my step-brother up and asked him and he told them what he did and it was time for me to go.

That night I was sent to live with my sister in Wenatchee, WA for the rest of 7th grade and part of 8th grade. She was going through a divorce and then remarried her ex-husband so I was sent back to Anacortes with my father, step-mother and my molester, my step-brother. I was happy to be reunited with some of my old girlfriends and joined every club in school so I wouldn't have to go home. I ironed shirts for fifteen cents a shirt, mowed lawns, anything I could do to earn money. I had a friend who was sixteen and I paid her to drive me to MT.

Vernon and I read my mom and dad's divorce papers and then asked to see a CPS worker to be put in an orphanage. I had my little bit of belongings packed and with me. Yes, my 45 records and little suitcase type record player. I was told I'd have to go back to my father's house while they investigated. Before Christmas a social worker showed up at the house and told me to pack my things she was taking me to my new home.

I quickly gathered my things and she took me to my foster parent's home, Erwin and Andrine Knapp, two teachers in Anacortes. They had three children and they gave me the first real home I had ever known. I am still in touch with them today and thank them for making me feel safe and like I do belong and I don't have to be afraid anymore.

At fifteen and 8 months old, yes I was still a baby but I had been engaged for a year and my boyfriend's father had to move back to Michigan to the VA hospital for the spider cancer he had. I made the choice to get married and move with them. His mother was a second mother to me and treated me like her daughter. It was a way for me to get emancipated. We were married in Anacortes on August 7th, 1961. Two weeks later we were living in Lincoln Park, Michigan the first married couple to go to school together. I was a junior and he was a senior. He was my first personal experience with physical abuse.

He was very controlling, womanizing, and egotistical guy. He would beat me just to beat me, I didn't have to say or do anything and he would hurt me in a minute so that made me very cautious and introverted. After six months, I snuck to a pay phone and called my father to send me a Greyhound ticket to get back to WA. He said no, so more beatings.

When my husband graduated and went in the Navy my senior year was great because he wasn't around. I graduated early and he got stationed in Millington, TN outside of Memphis, he had found a house in Munford, TN a tiny town eleven miles from base. He was too active with the ladies to have a wife living anywhere he was doing his thing. In 1963 he got orders to report to San Diego, CA and at that point we had already decided to divorce but he was still beating me. On my last night in TN, we were staying with some friends with the U-haul loaded and he tried to trade me to the husband and him the wife. That's when I took off and went to Graceland and ended up picking blades of grass from Elvis's yard which I still have. I was seventeen and yes I jumped the fence!

It was 1963 the guard came out and talked to me as I was quite emotional and Elvis was away making a movie so he told me to go to a Catholic church that was open all night and I would be safe. I did go there and a priest came out and comforted me and I slept in the pew. The next morning I went back to hook up the U-haul and told my husband I'm leaving if your coming with me get in the car.

We stopped in California for a week to see his mother and grandparents then drove to my father's property where he had a camper set up for me to live in. He was onto his third wife and again I was not allowed in the house except to shower. I had not let my husband touch me sexually for months and the last night he attacked me and that is when my daughter was conceived. The next morning I dropped him off at the bus station to go to California and I applied for jobs on the way home. Woolworths had called before I got from Mt. Vernon to Sedro Woolley and I started work the next day. I was the fountain lunch counter girl.

I missed two of my periods and knew I didn't have protection when he attacked me in the camper so I knew I was pregnant. I didn't tell anyone, my father noticed I was starting to show and he called my mother-law in California, and told her he thought I was pregnant and next thing I know she is moving back to Anacortes and I'm to go be roommates with her and get out of the camper and away from my dad and new step-mother so of course when her son/my husband got stationed at Whidbey Island and I was six months pregnant he came home to his mother's apartment and me too.

We decided to reconcile and I had my daughter on Feb, 27, 1964. We stayed together until she was six weeks old and he continued to beat and control me. He got order's to go to Okinawa and that is when my mother-in-law and her new husband showed up to take me and my daughter back to California with

13

them while he was away. I still had to pay the rent and utilities on the house we rented when he was deployed. My brother-in-law and sister-in-law came and took me out to my anniversary dinner corsage and all. They were the best man and maid of honor at my wedding in 1961.

They proceeded to tell me my husband was living with another woman in Okinawa and may have a child on the way. I moved out of my mother-in-laws and into a friend of mine a couple with three boys being the live in nanny and house keeper. I disappeared and no one knew where my daughter and I were. When my husband flew into the naval base from Okinawa I was there with my daughter to tell him I had packed up the house and shipped it to California. That I was filing for divorce, he got a motel and that is when he beat me up so bad and held a gun to me in every orifice and surface of my body with my daughter in the room.

The next day he called the old landlord and got the rental house back, he then locked and nailed all exits from the house and went to the train station to try to retrieve everything I had packed and shipped. Luckily the train had already left the station. When he was gone I broke a window got my daughter and ran to the neighbors when I called my step brother who had molested me and told him you owe me get us to the airport. He did pick us up and get us to Sea-Tac before my husband could catch us. My husband said he would have caught up with us but he had a flat tire on the way. I have never been as relieved as went that plane took off and I landed in California.

Little did I know that my husband would go AWOL come and find us? He talked me into going for a drive with him to talk over the divorce. Big mistake, he took me to a mountain raped and beat me and left me naked. I used leaves to cover myself and got down off that mountain to the first house and they gave me clothes to put on and the military police picked him up. He was in the brig for quite some time. He filed for divorce in WA. My daughter and I flew up to WA for the final decree and it was postponed he was in the Navy hospital with the mumps. My father had driven my daughter and me to see my husband in the hospital so he could see his daughter. My father was so drunk and driving he scraped the rock cliff driving back to Sedro Woolley. My daughter was in the car so I reached over and shut the car off and took the keys and told him I was driving the rest of the way. Things got a little heated between him and I and I drove and left to go back to California the next day.

When we got back to California and the couple I was the live in nanny for helped me get on my feet and get my own apartment. I worked at a donut shop. One day I looked out the window of the shop and I saw my father's pick-up and camper. He wouldn't come in the shop so I went out and knocked on the camper door and asked what he was doing here. He said my mother-in-law sent him to check on me and my daughter that she wanted to take my daughter from me. No, my divorce had not been finalized yet. There was no reason for the threat of taking my daughter from me she was my first priority. I received no child support and worked extra hours to support us.

My father followed me to my daycare for my daughter when I picked her up a block from my apartment. He came in and checked out the apartment and could find nothing wrong. It was clean and food in the cupboards and refrigerator he then went back out to his camper and left the next morning before I left for work. That is the last time I saw my father or spoke to him. He died 12/10/1970 passed out in a house fire along with his 4th wife.

My, mother-in-law, my sister and my father were all in cahoots to take my daughter from me. I didn't let them control me. In 1965 my daughter and I moved back to Washington and reconnected with my sister. I worked at a local restaurant and lived a block away. A friend from the restaurant took me out to the Space Needle for dinner, I was served Hay Stack's they tasted like fruit juice and had alcohol in them. I was nineteen; the ride down in the elevator was quite interesting as I wasn't a drinker, my friend then took me on the tram over the waterfall and to where he worked at Wonder Bread in Seattle for a tour. One thing led to another and we had sex. It was the only time in a year and then I found out I was pregnant. My divorce was not final from my daughter's father so my sister shipped me back to Wenatchee and told no one I was expecting.

In 1965-66 it was like a scarlet letter. I had no shame I looked on it that he was a blessing from God, but I was not to keep him. I had him in my room and took pictures and talked to him to know how I wanted him and loved him and he would always be in my heart. A private adoption was arranged. To this day I cannot watch the movie Sophie's Choice where Meryl Streep had to choose between her son and daughter in the concentration camp. I had called my sister and begged to let me come back with both my children and she would not budge. Again someone was controlling my life and not in a nice way.

After I returned with my daughter to my sister's in Lynnwood I was an emotional mess. After giving up my son I had shut down. Of course my sister introduced me to a fellow trucker and decided we should get married. I just went along with it. I felt I had no voice and my joy was gone. She went with Jim to get the rings, dress, shoes the whole outfit, reception hall I literally was not involved. She even invited my father. Jim was a truck driver so my daughter & I only saw him a couple weeks after we were married.

Two weeks before my twenty-first birthday my daughter and I were sent to California for a two week vacation so her grandmother could see her. Little did I know it was to get me out of town for a big surprise 21st birthday party with all the relatives and friends at another banquet room? My mother-in-law double crossed my sister and talked me into looking for a job and if I found one to stay in California. Of course I found a job and started working and never went back to WA. Until 1975! The marriage was annulled I mailed back the diamond wedding rings and began my life in California.

I married Ray, he was eleven years older than me and had four children with his first wife and the kids lived with us. I got pregnant and had a miscarriage a baby boy at five months pregnant. We bought a four bedroom house with a pool in San Jose. I was working as a cocktail waitress in Los Gatos. Ray became very jealous and if I was five minutes late getting home he would be waiting to attack and beat me. I took my daughter and ran to a motel. Eventually I would go back. I left him the night I was taking my daughter to go camping at her grandma's cabin in Williams, OR. I didn't come back except to get my daughters and my personal belongings.

That night I left and had dropped my daughter off at her grandma's for vacation I stopped by a girlfriends of mine and she talked me into going out to the Red Coach with her. I was going to go to Reno and get a quickie divorce. She ended up talking me into being her roommate. She had three boys. I started working at the Jamaican Inn, in Sunnyvale and would stop by the Red Coach when I got off to listen to the band the Tow Away Zone. I was breaking up with a boyfriend as he was abusive and controlling also. The guys in the Tow Away Zone were Howard, keyboard Billy, drums, and Chuck on guitar. Later Chuck was replaced with Ed Gibson on the Sax.

On the week-ends they would break down and set up playing after hours in Fremont south of San Francisco. The big acts that came to play at the Fairmont Hotel in San Francisco would go to Fremont for after hours and set in and play with the Tow Away Zone. I got to meet some famous entertainers.

Little did I know Howard had his eye on me? He came to my house one night and we were together body, mind and soul. We moved into a duplex and started our life together. Howard introduced me to myself with unconditional love and joy. He put the air beneath my wings. In 1974 we took a vacation to Washington to visit my sister and her family. Sue, my daughter stayed with my sister when Howard and I went to Victoria, BC for four days. He met my mother and we took her camping. He was so sweet to my mom and she fell in love with him at first glance.

Not long after we got back to the bay area from vacation my sister called and said Mom could come live with me that since my dad had died she was not nervous or terrorized any longer. Howard and I both said yes, she could come live with us. My sister disagreed about her moving to California and I needed to leave Howard and move back to Washington to have her come live with my daughter and me. She was not allowed to live with my sister and her husband as they had been part of the problem back in 1953. Howard knew the separation between my mom and me all those years that needed to be healed and he loved me enough to let me go. He is the only man that did not beat me.

We stayed in contact and vacationed together until he died on my birthday in 2012. He is the only man I ever loved or felt his unconditional love for me.

August 1975 my daughter and I moved back to Washington and I proceeded to go through the process of my mom moving in with us. During that time my sister set me up with Doug a friend of theirs, we ended up married for three years. He had been a Caption in the Army during the Viet Nam war. He would beat me, black eyes and broken jaw, threw me though the picture glass window almost slitting my throat. There were no domestic violence laws at that time. He didn't need a reason to hurt me he just chalked it up to Viet Nam flashbacks.

My mom moved to a fancy retirement center and my daughter and I moved into a townhouse. I was then offered a Certified Instructor position with the phone company and moved to Beaverton, OR for eight years. When in Oregon I married Jon that was so short lived it was annulled. He was also an abuser; he would beat me and lock me out of the house. He threw tree rounds not split for the fire at me and the car. Tried to run me over with my car and he stalked me and would not sign the divorce papers.

In 1984 I moved back to Washington and filed for divorce, I had to publish in his local newspaper for six weeks that I was divorcing him. He made no response so my divorce was finalized. I paid for a separate name change to Evans. I just wanted to be

M.E. Since 1957 all the kids in my life called me, MeMe.

From 1984 to 2003 I remained single and did a lot of work and counseling on myself. I would date but if they got to serious I'd back off. I retired from the phone company in 1996 after 20 ½ years and then I went into insurance.

June 19, 2001 I moved to Nokomis, FL. My old phone company boss and his wife retired there. I got a job in Workman Comp. in Sarasota. I had leased a park model with a Florida room at Encore Resort in Nokomis. It was really fun living there, especially when the snowbirds from the east coast came November to June. I loved the pool parties every Sunday, music, sunshine and BBQ. I had met Donald at the Saltwater Café one Friday night when I stopped after work for lobster pizza. He was much younger than me but we became friends and Kenny Smith the guitar player and his family became friends of mine.

After I had known Donald for six months he wanted introduce me to his older brother Ernie. Finally on February 17, 2002, I met Ernie he was going to be going to meet his granddaughter in Texas for the first time and my daughter and grandchildren were coming to visit me in Florida for three weeks over Easter. When Ernie got back from Texas he hung around with us and Donald and Ernie went parasailing with us right before we were to leave to the airport to get them back to Seattle. Come to find out the reason Donald wanted me to me Ernie is he

21

lived at home with his parents after his wife died waiting for a kidney and they needed house tax money to the tune of $1,300.00.

I had saved up enough money to get me a new computer but with an elderly couple losing their home I could not in good conscious spend that money on a computer for me. I paid their house taxes and they still did a reverse mortgage. Ernie and Donald were just guys that were my friends. I was dating other people.

I had been in counseling since I was forty and single for twenty years so was not looking for any serious relationship. Ernie knew where I kept my extra key outside incase I locked myself out. After three months of being friends and buddy's I woke up with him naked in my bed. I had a six month rule no intimacy until I've known you for six month. He broke that rule but was always a gentleman to me and I could see a moral man in him.

In July of 2002 we flew to Texas to see his granddaughter. I fell in love with her at first site and she has grown into a beautiful smart young lady. We got back from Texas and everything continued as normal. In Dec of 2002 I told him I was moving to Las Vegas, I had transferred with Workman Comp. He then talked me into staying one more year. We would get a house and he was moving in. I moved into the house Jan. 1, 2003 he moved in 2/27/2003, he had always asked me to marry him but I thought it was a joke. He wore me down and on March 8, 2003 we were married. Once I signed that marriage certificate I began to see another side of him like him calling me his dead wife's name, before we were married he knew my name. Not being available to me.

I worked two jobs from 8AM to 12 midnight. When I got off Workman Comp I then went to work at Bed Bath and Beyond. He would take my new car to go out when I was working and forget to pick me up after work so I'd have to walk over a mile home after midnight. He felt he was entitled to free rent. I had fallen off a ladder and had a claim, I got my settlement so we bought the van loaded a small u-haul and headed back to Washington. We arrived June 4, 2004. We lived in a RV park for a year because we didn't know where he would get a job. Getting him to find a job or work was a real issue. I worked at Staples.

The physical abuse started in 2005 where he called it Tinker Belling me by picking me up and throwing me on the bed to shut up and lay there. Christmas of 2004 we went to see his daughter and her first husband and now two grandchildren in Anchorage Alaska. She had her second girl in Alaska February 4, 2004. They took us to a lodge for the night and when his daughter and son-in-law went down to the bar and I was finished taking a shower after swimming with the girls. I was tired and getting the girls in bed and he wasn't talking to me. I told him if he wanted to go, drink with his daughter go ahead and that is when he gave me a bloody nose in front of is granddaughters. He then left the room. No one spoke to me after that and when we returned to their base housing I was told to go upstairs and stay there. The girls and I played with all their new toys and I tried not to let them feel the tension. Early the next morning, when everyone was sleeping as they had stayed up late partying with friends over.

I snuck the phone and went outside and called my daughter to change my ticket and get me on the next plane out. She did and I flew home to her house that day. Ernie stayed for another week. January of 2005 we rented our apt in Arlington and going down the steps I fell and broke my ankle. I wore a boot for a long time. With boot and all I got a job two blocks from our apt. at the Arlington Times Newspaper. I worked the copy center until I retired full time. In 2007 was the next assault, this time raging at me for asking him to sign his daughter's birthday card so I could mail her box. He tore the card up and threw it in the garbage and grabbed me and started to yank me around and block the door so I couldn't get out and took the phone. I got the extra phone and called 911 he was arrested and charged with DV assault and false imprisonment. He was given DV classes to take and DV woman's group sharing their stories. All ordered by the court. I paid the court cost and the classes he had to take. 2010 this time slapping my face and pushing me into the corner of a counter the police were called again and he was arrested. This time I paid court cost, probation, and DV group counseling every week. I started going to counseling every week just to learn how to control my response to his moods, rages and his disassociation with me. He admitted he resented me going to counseling and would take it out on me every week when I came home.

He would always block the exit door and keep raging and spiting in my face and holding me down on the bed trying to crush my jaw and head butting me. He would always get arrested for DV Imprisonment because he would not let me get away from him or his abuse. His silence would speak volumes to me. I became his care taker and supporter putting a roof over his head and feed him. July of 2014 we took a trip to Texas to see his daughter, new husband and grandkids; everything was fine until the sixth day when all heck broke out between his daughter and himself. She called the police he was not arrested and we left for the airport in Dallas a day early. Luckily we got on standby so we didn't have to wait the sixteen hours before our scheduled flight would take off. I cried on the flight all the way home I knew that he just took my granddaughters away from me after being the only grandma they ever knew. When we got home from Texas in 2014 he did the same abuse as was his routine, this time when he was arrested he went to SCORE in Des Moines for six weeks. He was released the day before Thanksgiving. He didn't have any where to go and I tried every mission anywhere where he would not have to come back here. I could not find a place that would accept him. I was planning on spending Thanksgiving with my daughter for the first time in four years.

My grandson came over that night and had a man to man talk with him and said he was coming to get me for Thanksgiving and Ernie wasn't invited after all the abuse he had done to his grandma. Ernie took it well and yes he got a plate of left over's so he had Thanksgiving dinner.

From July to December 22, 2015 he went to his court ordered counseling and he lied to the counselor. On December 22nd I was setting in my computer chair and started to discuss a menu I had on a t-shirt-sweatshirt and my winter coat on as I was going to walk down and get me some M&M candy. Before I could do anything he jumped off the couch and grabbed and threw me on the bed. He put me in a wrestler's hold where I could not move. He proceeded to smother me until I passed out an couldn't breathe I passed out that's what made him stop and I took a grasp of breath, all the time head butting me and trying to crush my jaw and smothering me to the point of passing out this went on for two and a half hours. I didn't think I was going to make it out of this one. He let the pressure off my left arm and I have a seven carat Tourmaline ring and swung and hit his forehead with the sharp part of the ring. He then let off my right arm to check where I had hit him with the ring and I took that opportunity to take both hands and scratch from his under eye down his face as hard as I could. He asked why did you do that & I replied leaving trace evidence. I told him I need to go put some cold water on my face. I have a heart valve problem and could hardly breathe. He dragged and pulled me into the bathroom threw me on the floor and poured a bucket of water on me. He then went into the kitchen next to the bathroom. I got myself up and dried off with a towel and put a cold rag on my face for awhile.

When I came out of the bathroom I still had my coat on and he started throwing all the knives out of my kitchen knife block at me twelve in all. I got cuts on my hands they were the only part that wasn't covered. He announced he had to go to the bathroom and threw me into the computer chair and said if I went to the police he'd make sure I went to jail also. As soon as I heard that first tinkle (men cannot stop their stream at that point) I got up and ran, I got across the street and saw the van out of the corner of my eye and ran like a sixteen year old (I'm 70) and had it unlocked ready to pull the handle and get in and go. Ernie came out at the top of the steps of the apt. He saw me getting in the van & yelled "go ahead take the van and walk back into the apt."

I drove immediately to the police station and asked for an officer. The officer interviewed me, took pictures of my injuries and had me write a statement. Ernie called my cell phone three times when I was with the officer I hung up on each one without saying a word. The officer had to wait for his partner to come and go to our apt to arrest Ernie. The police report stated he would not say a word just "take me to jail" he thought he was going to go back to SCORE the campus type jail but he got booked into the Snohomish County Jail on Dec. 22, 2015. We offered him a 180 days jail time, a five year protection order and probation. His attorney offered 120 days time served no protection order or probation. Of course the prosecuting attorney did not agree with that. In fact he called me and asked what is wrong with that man he is a chronic abuser. I had already gotten the paper work together to file for divorce. Ernie decided to go for jury trial on March 15th and I was subpoenaed to appear and testify.

On March 6th he was served with my divorce papers and decided against the jury trial and let the judge sentence him. He got 364 days on March 15th no credit for time served since Dec.22.2015, I have my own protection order that is good until 2/7/1017 and I will be renewing that three months before it expires and I have all the previous police reports to get a five year protection order. I'm on a waiting list to move into some secure apartments. I have packed all of his belongings and put them in his storage as the divorce indicated. His daughter and her husband came from Texas to get all her childhood memories, pictures and keepsakes and her Mom's ashes.

I cannot explain the load that was lifted off my shoulders when I walked out of the court house with my final divorce papers in hand.

I am free I had my life and voice back. No more abuse or being silenced. No more walking on egg shells or full of stress just to get through the day. He was never my friend or boyfriend or husband.

No more than I wasn't his bride, wife or friend. I believed in him and as long as he was trying I stood by him for fourteen years. I guess it took me that long to learn the lesson. I am less alone without him than when I was with him. I have a life now and it's wonderful even if it did take me seventy years to be my authentic self. I know who I am and that's a great feeling.

The last fourteen years was when there was a domestic law to protect the victim. Be prepared to divorce immediately or get ready to spend some money for your abusers actions. It cost me $100,000.00 in fourteen years. Domestic Violence and abuse is not free. You're paying your abuser to abuse you.

At 10:00 PM August 23rd, 2016 I receive a call from the Snohomish County Jail to inform me that my Ex-husband would be released within four to six hours. I asked why, I was told the jail is to full. I was being informed early in case I needed to take any precautions. Excuse me I thought he was in jail and sentenced to 364 days didn't do me justice with 118 days served. I was not expecting that early of a release I thought December maybe. I had a twenty-two hour melt down of shaking and crying that without my neighbors especially Travis Milan who stayed with me and Jody Doty who sent me calming meditations and the prayer chains started by Jody and Leisa Evans. In the mean time my ex-stepdaughter was having a fit because I put a picture of her father my ex who I have the protection order against him that he was out early and if he was in Old Town Arlington he was within the range of breaking the protection order. She proceeded to hack my page and remove the prayer chains and anything related to her father. I reported her to Facebook, changed my password and blocked her and un-friended her. Then the phone started to blow up and she was screaming at me and said she did want to hear another F-ing word from my mouth again so each time she called back I calmly said you don't want to her another word from by mouth good-bye... the phone calls from her have stopped. Then just this Tuesday I get a call from Community Health about my ex-husbands health insurance. The one he applied for apparently after being realized from jail. I would of thought nothing of the call if had come in on the house phone but it came on my cell phone which was for emergencies only and never given as a contact number as it was the pay as you go. Only my ex could have given them that number. It's probably the only number he could remember. That lets me know he's still in the area. To keep my guard up and get the law changed to three strikes you out if it's physical or a Felony.

This is the law now the court makes money the system makes money and the woman is not protected.

§ In addition to jail or prison time, you could face penalties including

§ Fines

§ Anger management classes

§ Counseling

§ Community service

Most states immediately require a domestic violence defendant to turn over any weapons they may own. This means you may <u>no longer lawfully possess a firearm</u> in most states.

In summary what I have learned from this experience is that the system is broken I was abused before there was a DV law and after the DV law was put on the books the only difference is that it cost me a lot of money for court cost, classes, counseling, probation and attorney fees. That is it the law should be changed to a felony or three strikes you're out especially if it is physical abuse. It took seven times in court for him to get jail time. I have no faith in the court system or the law that is in place. This last time it was so bad that he finally got jail time that allowed me to get a divorce and protection order before he got out. He only served 118 days of a 364 day sentence. Again more money spent just to protect myself. The most dangerous time is when you're getting out and I managed that and have my life back to where I am free. I wear maze on me at all times and have taken self defensive classes. I am not going to go through this world looking over my shoulder and being fearful I have taken my power back. I walk freely on this earth full of wonderful people and joy. It doesn't matter how old you are, how rich you are if you are being abused you have to get away from your abuser.

Except for my last husband of fourteen years I always left when it got physical. I tolerated the emotional, mental and verbal abuse and it wasn't easy I learned to detach and keep my spirit. No one was going to steal my soul I am 71 and have done thirty-one years of professional counseling to keep myself whole. It gave me an outlet to speak my mind without judgment and to get tools of how I responded to the abuse. It was worth every penny I spent on myself. I was single for twenty years and my ex-husbands were all charming and gentlemen until I signed that marriage license. It's like a pedophile they groom you until it's to0 late and you're in too deep. I can tell you it will never get better only worse I'd rather be respected than loved. If you have someone not treating you right you know it you feel it even if it's not physical. Get out now before it gets worse... no man is worth your time if he can abuse you in any way.

I have always been very independent and not afraid to go it on my own. I now know that is my path in life. I married for love not money but because I had a career and held up my part it became an issue. Maybe it intimidated my husband's that I made more money than they did. It wasn't an issue for me because I looked at my marriages as a partnership but they obviously didn't.

If my story can save one woman then it was all worth it. Don't let it be your life lesson you may end up dead. I have permanent scars from the beatings and broken jaws but I am alive and enjoying my life and the time I have left. Even if you have to go to a shelter get out. There is help out there to get you back on your feet. Walk away from anything material and save yourself. Your life is important. You are living in fear and stress and that takes its toll on your physical health. If children are involved they will continue the circle of abuse break that circle now before it is too late for their future in this world. Abuse will become their comfort zone and affect their future. Mom and Dad acted that way so they think it's normal, even when they are trembling with fear to see their mother beaten. It teaches your daughters and sons this is how relationships work and they will choose an abuser and it will continue in the family until you yes you walk away and get help. You have the power to do that and only you can do it. Remember you can only control yourself not anyone else. Call the Domestic Hotline and make an exit plan. Mine was to get to the fire station a block from my apartment where I would be behind their locked facility where he couldn't get me I had a number to call no name and would be picked up at the fire station and taken to a safe house or shelter. I was willing to walk away with the clothes on my back because I choose life. Please for you and your children's sake make the leap of faith that you can live better without your abuser.

There is no more cry left.
There is relief and joy.
There is peace of mind.
There is lack of stress.
There is hope.
No one can steal my soul.
God protects me and loves me.
I pray I learned the lessons this life holds.
I have put a lot of living into my seven decades.
I plan to live in the moment and to the very end of life on this earth.
I am a enabler I will give you enough rope to hang yourself all the time thinking I'm being understanding and having empathy to your needs and conditions all the time hurting myself because I forget me.
When you have no more to give you are empty.
You don't want to be more alone with someone that without them in your life.
You think about the woman you want to be the life, you want and make it happen. You're a woman you can do it. Look at all you have endured and survived and now it's time to thrive in whatever that means to you. Find yourself again , this experience has changed you look at what it taught you and jump for joy you don't have to be hurt anymore and you can be anything you want.

I feel contented, joy, grateful, and blessed. It was worth all the effort and time to be free.

What do I think of this new found freedom? Contentment;

My new adventure is the excitement of rediscovering myself and life again.

To be myself is refreshing and rewarding.

I have healed and moved on and looking forward to this new chapter.

About the author: My name is Wade Bloodgood. I am an Oregon native. I am 41 years young. I am a father, a certified speaker, an outdoor survival instructor, entrepreneur, and an avid fisherman. I have a deep love for nature. Among my favorite things to do is to spend time with my dog, Seeley. My goal and purpose in life is to bring growth, peace and healing to anyone wanting to overcome the suffering of internalized childhood and adulthood issues.

Acknowledgments: I would like to start by thanking Kellie Fitzgerald for giving me this opportunity to tell one of the most impacting of my life's stories. I am grateful and appreciate you very much, Kellie. I would like to thank my editor, Tony Dodd. He has been a good friend for over a decade, and is one of the most talented and intelligent people I know. He can take my rambling writings and turn them into true literary beauty. Not an easy task! :) You are appreciated. I would like to thank my son for being born and for being a blessing in my life! I am grateful, love, and appreciate you, DaVannis! I'd like to convey huge thanks, appreciation, and gratitude to my best friend, Carolyn Clow and her boys, for all the love, and for being such a huge part of my growth. You have taught me what a true friend is, and what it means to be family. You truly are the Dali Mama. Thank you to everyone that has stood by my side, even when it wasn't easy. I appreciate all of you for not giving up on me!

When I was offered the opportunity to tell my story of abuse, and to share my journey of suffering, survival, and eventually; thriving, I didn't know where to start. There are so many events that have painted the picture of my life. This is one life story that had a tremendous impact on making me the man that I have since become.

When I was 7 years old, living in Portland, Oregon, my biological father (Jimmy) left my mother (Linda), my brother (Heath) and I for another woman. He was physically and verbally abusive. His departure was a blessing, but that's not what this story is about. It was his familial abandonment that allowed the events that followed.

Within a year, my mother started dating again. She met a man named Eugene, and after a few months, they began dating exclusively. Everyone called him Gene. Gene was a really good guy. He treated my mother with love and respect. He played guitar, and loved to play and sing Beatles songs. He was a photographer, and possessed many other trade skills that eventually led him into the home repair business. Everyone loved Gene. Family, friends, neighborhood kids...He got along with everyone. He was the "life of the party" type of guy. He had a daughter who was a year older than me. I had a new friend, and eventually, a stepsister. She lived with her mother full-time, but would often visit us.

Gene was nothing like my father. He never yelled at us. He never physically abused my mother. He was not a drug addict or alcoholic. He took us hiking and camping; a lot of outdoor stuff. Gene and my mom dated for about two and a half years before moving in together. Eighteen months later, Gene and my mother told me that we were moving.

Gene had relatives in Hawaii, and was offered a job there. We were moving from Oregon to Oahu, and life for me was going to quickly change. All I knew as "family," and all of my friends, lived in Oregon. I was afraid of the move. Hawaii was a foreign place to me. I was not sure where I would fit in, or if I would fit in at all. I was 11 years old. I had always been a tall, skinny, lanky kid; emotionally sensitive and hyperactive. I had a lot of emotional issues, due to the first seven years of abuse; emotional, physical, and verbal abuse from a father that ruled by fear. I needed a lot of attention and I sought it in many different ways. Even at such a young age, I had a severe sense of inadequacy. I felt that I was not good enough. I thought that my dad left because he didn't love us. I felt abandoned in that area and my stepfather was filling his shoes, but only doing so because that came as a package deal with my mother; As if he really didn't want that role or responsibility. He wanted to be more of a friend than a father figure or role model in my life. Gene made things fun.

When we arrived in Hawaii, for the first few months, we lived with Gene's brother. My mother and Gene were now married. We moved into a five-bedroom house with another of his brothers and his family. To me, it felt like we were rich. I had always felt that we were white trash; between lower class and poverty level. In Oregon, there were times when there was very little in the house to eat. In Hawaii, we lived in a big house, with a huge yard, next to a City Park to play in. We always had plenty of food to eat, and for once in my life, I had no real worries. I had my own bedroom, and my own bed. I felt safe.

Gene's family became my new family. Suddenly, I had new aunts, uncles, cousins, and grandparents. They all treated me with love: love that I desperately needed at that time. They provided me with the attention that I had been seeking. Previously, I would do things solely for attention, and it didn't matter whether those things were positive or negative. It didn't matter, because to me, any attention was SOME attention, and any attention was better than NO attention. Even if I was punished, I somehow perceived that to mean that I was loved. My new family and home environment brought a newfound positive attitude, with the love of family and simple kindness. They will never know how much that meant to me. The impact that their love has made upon my life is immeasurable. I can vividly remember, decades later, that at 11 years old, for the first time in my life, I was happy.

After living in our new house for a few months, we finally settled in. One day, my new stepfather suggested that we should all go camping. My mom wasn't feeling well, and said that she did not want to go. My older brother, at 15 years old, really didn't want much to do with anyone. In fact, he was very vocal about wanting to move back to Oregon and live with our "real" family. When he was asked to go camping, he immediately declined. It looked like it was just going to be Gene and me.

We would be camping overnight at a place only accessible by a downhill trail named Heart Attack Hill. The hike in was downhill. The short, but very steep trail led to three waterfalls, with large pools underneath each one. The most popular is known as Waimano Pool. It is located at the end of Pacific Palisades in Pearl City. Many people jump into the pools from the cliffs above. It was a short hike off the main path, and only those that know the trail normally go down to these waterfalls to the secluded spot. It's not a place that people usually camp, but instead a swimming hole for day-hikers.

The steep hike is not heavily traveled, and we quickly made our way to the bottom of the trail to set up camp. Once we arrived at the waterfalls, we saw the three big pools. Each one was connected to the other, and there was a small mound of dirt at the edge of the main pool. This is where we decided to camp. Within ten minutes, our campsite was set up. We decided to explore, and climbed the hill to the top of the waterfall.

Once at the top, we walked up the stream that preceded the waterfall, gathering tropical fruits like guava, mango, and mountain apples. We made our way back to camp, and instead of climbing down the trail, we jumped off the cliff into the pool, and swam back to our campsite. We continued to swim in the pools most of the day, escaping the heat of the scorching sun overhead. As night approached, we ate some sandwiches and started a small fire. About twenty minutes after the sunset, Gene went into his backpack and pulled out a pipe and a bag of marijuana. Even though I was only 11 years old, I had been smoking pot with friends and older friends of my brother (who is four years older than me), since I was 8 years old. Side note: When I was 5 years old, my biological father used to blow marijuana smoke in my face; an action that I recall to this day. My point is that even at eleven, I was very familiar with the Hippie Lettuce.

Gene had known that my brother and I were smoking marijuana for quite some time, but he had never mentioned it, except to tell us to never steal it from him. He had never offered to smoke with me, mainly because he knew my mother's stance on the subject. She didn't condone illegal drug use, and condemned any adult-action that contributed to the delinquency of minors in any way, shape, or form. Gene turned to me and said, "I'll smoke with you, but you have to promise to never tell your mom." Of course, I agreed to his terms. We smoked a couple of bowls of really good Hawaiian pot, and shortly thereafter, I was super stoned. We hung out, and watched the stars for about an hour. We decided to call it a night, and crawled into the tent. I quickly drifted off to sleep, to the soothing sound of the waterfall crashing just feet from where I lay.

I abruptly woke up in the middle of the night. Gene was touching my penis. I was in shock, and completely terrified. Frozen with fear, I begin to whimper and cry. Gene told me it was okay. He continued touching me, as he told me about his cousin in the Philippines that did the same thing to him when he was a kid, and that it was perfectly normal. I knew right away that it was not normal. As a child, I was taught the "run yell and tell" program from my mother, and in school assemblies. My mother also taught us to cover our nudity and that it wasn't something that we showed others. This occurred after knowing, respecting, and loving my stepfather for over four years. I never suspected that Gene would ever do this. After he finished telling me about being touched as a child, he finally stopped. Still crying, and still stoned, I cried myself back to sleep.

When I woke in the morning, I was relieved to see that Gene was not in the tent. I looked out the zippered door, and saw Gene standing on the edge of the water. He was completely nude, with an erection, and was masturbating. I immediately pulled myself back into the tent, and began feverishly considering what options I had to remove myself from the situation. I decided to just walk out, and go up the hill as fast as I could. When I came out of the tent Gene saw me, put his shorts on, and told me that we were staying another night. He said that we needed to go gather more fruit and demanded that we go together, immediately. I honestly believed there was a chance that he was going to kill me. I didn't try to run.

Instead, I decided to wait for the right opportunity to make my escape.

Gene adopted an angry and agitated attitude. This was not normal behavior for him. Neither he nor I mentioned what had happened in the tent the night before. After gathering fruit, we returned to camp and sat around for several hours. Nothing was said. We didn't look at each other. Gene decided he was going to disassemble some rocks that were creating a dam effect on one of the lower waterfall pools, to raise the water level. As he was doing this, I asked if I could go up the hill to the main trail and go back to the car fir something. At first, he was adamantly opposed to the idea. An hour later, I asked again, and he angrily told me that I could, but reminded me that I would have to find my way back by myself. The instant he said that I could leave. I was running up Heart Attack Hill back to the main trail as fast as my legs and heart would take me. Ten minutes later, I made my way to the main trail. I noticed some hikers walking towards me. As they walked past, I said nothing, and ran all the way back to the parking area, which was located at the end of a street in a residential neighborhood.

When I reached the car, I decided that I was not going to return to the campsite. Instead, I would wait for Gene to come up and drive me home. I was so nervous. I sat and cried on the curb. I waited for hours. I just wanted to be with my mother and brother. After waiting several hours, I noticed an elderly man working in his yard down the street. I walked up to him, and explained that my step-dad had not returned from hiking. I asked if I could use his telephone to call my mother. He took me inside to his telephone and stood there as I dialed the number. When my mother answered, once I heard her voice, I immediately started crying. She asked me if there was something wrong. Had something happened? I didn't want to tell her the truth with the man standing next to me, so I told her that Gene didn't return from hiking, that he wanted to camp another night, and that I just wanted to come home. She told me that someone would be there to get me as soon as possible.

Forty-five minutes later, as the sun was beginning to set, Gene exited the trail and was quickly walking towards me. He was furious. He yelled at me, and told me that he only allowed me to come to the car if I could return to the campsite by myself. He was angry because he wanted to stay another night. He told me to get in the car. I complied. Sheepishly, I told him that my Grandpa and Uncle were coming to get me. Before he could react, they pulled up right beside us. I instantly jumped into the safety of their car. They both recognized my fear. Gene yelled to them, "You take him home! I'll meet you at the house" and peeled off in his car, with tires screeching.

Grandpa and Uncle took me home. Even though Gene left before us, we arrived at the house before he did. My mother and my brother were standing in the driveway. Grandpa stopped, waved, and let me out. I ran to my mother and brother. I was relieved to see them, and started crying and hyperventilating. My mom asked if there was something wrong. Between tears and deep breaths, I told them that Gene had touched me on my private parts. My brother said, "I'm going to kill that motherfucker." Mom told us to calm down and said to wait to react until the entire story was told. "We don't even know what's really going on here," she said.

At that moment, Gene pulled into the driveway. Mom sent Heath and me to our rooms. I could hear Gene yelling, "Your kids will say anything to break us up. I would never touch a kid." They argued for hours. When the fighting finally ended, my mother came into my room. She said that Gene told her that he never touched me. He said that he was only massaging my legs when I was sleeping because I was complaining that my legs hurt from hiking; that what I thought happened was actually just a dream. I cried to her and tried to explain that it really did happen. **IT HAPPENED. IT HAPPENED. HE TOUCHED ME. HE TOUCHED ME. PLEASE BELIEVE ME, MOM!**

She told me to calm down and reminded me that what happened was not real; that it was only a dream. Gene would never touch me in that way. He would never do anything like that. At that moment, I had never felt more alone. To this day, I have never felt more abandoned. I felt like I was not loved, and that I could never be loved. How could the woman that taught me how to "run, yell and tell" not believe me when I ran, yelled and told? I felt like I was on fire. I was "stop, dropping and rolling" but the flames would not extinguish. For the second night in a row, I cried myself to sleep.

After that day, Gene started referring to me as "a piece of shit." He was no longer nice to me. He didn't want anything to do with me, and of course, I wanted nothing to do with him. Actually, what I wanted was to die. Nobody was there to protect me. Nobody gave a fuck about me except my brother, and within one week of the incident, he returned to Oregon to live with the family. I was completely alone, with no one to stand up for me. We stayed in Hawaii for another 6 months, until some of Gene's family in Las Vegas told him they would give him some work if he moved there. So, my parents packed up my life again, and off to Las Vegas we went. Another drastic life change.

I hated Las Vegas. Immediately, it felt like we were back at poverty level. Nobody liked me. My parents acted as if I wasn't even there. I had no friends. The only good thing about Las Vegas is that we only lived there for a year. Soon after, we moved back to Oregon. Gene and my mother separated soon after. That lasted a few months, until they reconciled. A year later, we moved back to Hawaii. Another drastic life change.

As a kid, we moved a lot and I had to go to a lot of different schools and adjust to making new friends. Trying to fit into new places, I never really felt like I fit in anywhere. I never really felt like I belonged. I was not a well-adjusted individual.

As I entered my teenage years, I continued to do more and more drugs. I became my biggest enemy I became my biggest abuser. I was a liar. I was a cheater. I was a thief. I was not proud of myself, but I didn't care. If no one else cares about me, why should I care about me? I was consumed with self-loathing. All of my actions and behavior were huge signs that something was wrong. I've always felt like I have been crying out for help, with the way I was acted, and still, nobody would come and save me. I felt like I did not matter to anyone. My biological father said that I could never be loved, that I'd never have a family, or amount to anything. His words became the truth within myself, regarding who I thought I was at that time and the perception of everything that I could never be.

Once we moved back to Hawaii, things seemed to improve, except my mental health. Gene was being nice to me. Mom was very happy, but I was still dealing with unresolved issues, and I was completely fucking miserable. All I wanted to do was die. Doing drugs was my slow way of doing it. Gene had a decent job and all of a sudden, he started acting very strangely again. It was as if he was a completely different person. Everybody was trying to figure out what was going on with him. It was almost as if he was going crazy. If you were to tell him that, he would act as if the person making the statement was the one that were crazy. Four months later, Gene and my mom separated again.

Gene was then diagnosed with manic depression and bipolar disease. They prescribed him Lithium to regulate his body chemicals. He was okay...for a while. He started making good money at his job. My mother and Gene reconciled. Again. My stepsister and her boyfriend moved to Hawaii, and we all moved into another five-bedroom house in a really nice neighborhood. At this time, Gene started doing drugs and wouldn't take his medication. One day, we decided to go to the beach for a family excursion, but Gene stayed behind. When we returned, our house was flooding water from the inside out. Gene had plugged all the drains, broke off all the toilets, and turned on all the faucets upstairs and downstairs. Water was pouring out of the house. That was the day we all became homeless.

With nowhere to go, we lived in the bushes on a beach that was on the outskirts of town. On the weekends, locals would party there and shoot guns. They didn't know that homeless people were living in the bushes. It was terrifying. My mother suffered from an extreme case of diabetes and also had Addison's Disease. She was very sensitive to sugar and was insulin dependent. She had to take a shot everyday to keep her body at acceptable levels, even when we were living in a tent. She had a diabetic seizure and fell into a coma. We took her to the hospital. When she came out of the coma, they kept her at the hospital for five days to recover. I hustled in any way I could to get money to get plane tickets back to Oregon to be with our family. My brother and his wife told me if we could get to Oregon, we could stay at their house for a while. When Mom got out of the hospital, I had already bought plane tickets and told her that we were flying back to Oregon. She didn't like the idea, but she didn't really have a choice because she was so sick. She reluctantly agreed.

Meanwhile, my stepfather was homeless, running around the island, doing God knows what. My stepsister and brother-in-law remained homeless for over a year, on that same beach, in the bushes, since I had only hustled enough money for me and my mom to get the hell out of there.

When we arrived in Oregon, my brother and his wife let us stay with them, but they lived in a one-bedroom apartment, so Mom and I were crashing on the sleeper sofa in the living room. My brother thought that my mother would go get a job, so that we could start looking for an apartment. She didn't. Mom fell into a massive depression, and everyday, she just laid on the couch, blaming me for bringing her to Oregon, and for Gene's mental problems. "This is all your fault, and there is nothing you can do to make me happy." She said she would rather be back in Hawaii dying, than being in Oregon. She was completely miserable.

After about four months of Mom lying on his couch, my brother told her that she needed to leave. Somehow, I managed to get us into a one-bedroom apartment. At this point, my mom could barely stand to look at me. She never really spoke to me. All she wanted was Gene back in her life. He was her world. Six months later, I got word that Gene was back in Oregon, and that he was no longer experiencing manic episodes. Though I didn't want my mom to get back with him, I decided it was time for me to give him a call, and beg him to come back and be with my mother She was so miserable with me, I thought there was no other option. And it was making me miserable as well. All I wanted from my mother was for her to love me. She didn't have love from Gene, and therefore could not love me. It was my fault.

On the phone, Gene was calm and friendly. He was surprisingly easy to talk to. He told me that he still loved my mother, and that he would love to go on a date with her, and perhaps rekindle their relationship. After that night, they reconciled. Again. Everything was great for them for about a year, when we moved to Hawaii. Again.

Five months after returning to the Island, Gene started acting strangely. For over a month, he hardly slept at all. One night, he woke me up in the middle of the night and asked me to help him rearrange all the furniture, so that he could be quiet and not wake my mother up. I knew right away that he was going crazy again. I didn't want my mom to find out, so I did all I could to help him keep up the charade that he was acting normally. I didn't want my mother to hate me for breaking her and Gene up (AGAIN), so I did whatever I could do to keep her happy, and keep her unaware of Gene's behavior. However, Gene's behavior was so over-the-top, eventually, I could no longer hide it. One day, he told me that he was going to leave my mom, and he asked me if he left her, would I come live with him. I told him to fuck off, and that I would never live with him.

I think I might have to kill my stepfather.

He became belligerent and told me that he was going to kill me. I left the house and ran down the road to nowhere in particular. I just wanted to be away from the situation. He got in his truck and literally chased me down. I ran on to the sidewalk to avoid being run over, and to my disbelief, he followed me onto the walkway, and accelerated. He was actually trying to run me over. I dove out of the way at the last moment, and missed being killed by mere inches. The police came and chased Gene around the block about seven times, and then several miles down county roads, before they were finally able to stop him. He was arrested and taken to jail. He was released the next day, and bought a plane ticket back to Oregon.

About four months later, my mother received a call from a family member. The caller told her that in the previous year, when she and Gene were broken up, that Gene went to California to visit his sister, and raped his nephew (my cousin) Brandon. When my mom heard this news, she didn't believe it. She wrote a letter to my cousin asking him if that actually happened. She got a letter in response that said only one word: YES. I remember that day vividly. I was 16 years old. She tearfully apologized to me for not believing that Gene had molested me. She tried to hug me, but I ran into the bathroom and locked the door. I fell to the floor and cried uncontrollably. At that moment, I hated my mother. She didn't believe me, and her inaction resulted in my cousin being raped. Instead of believing me, her son, she believed a man had "only" touched me, but in reality, was potentially going to rape me as well, if I had not "yelled and told " years earlier. I always felt it was my mom's job to "run, yell and tell" for me to the police, but instead, she convinced me that it was all a dream.

In the three years after Gene molested me, he did the same to at least one other boy, and he also repeatedly raped my cousin. I've always felt guilty about the people who were abused after I was, but I did what I was taught to do. Others didn't do what they should have done. Including, and perhaps most to blame, my mother. Other people were hurt; a lifetime of hurt. Brandon will never be the same, and I'm doing my best to rebuild my life from the very many broken pieces that created the person I believed I was. Who knows how many other unknown victims has he left in his wake?

It would be fourteen years before I saw Gene again. I was 31 years old, living in Florida, running my own business. I was drinking like a fish, and popping prescription drugs like they were breath mints. I was doing cocaine and pretty much whatever drugs were on the table. I've basically taken this route in life...as a loser. I was miserable and I was still living to die, since I was eight years old...but I began to question why I was doing this to myself? What caused me to take this route?

This caused me to do some serious introspection/retrospection and what I surmised is that all my issues and demons led back to my biological father, my stepfather, and my mother. Being molested, and then telling my mother, and not being believed is high on my "I'm Not Good Enough" Top Ten list.

I immediately decided to get off hard drugs. I chose to only smoke pot and drink alcohol to ease the detox of quitting prescription drugs. That took me ten weeks. Ten weeks of emotional, living death. Virtual hell. Everyday, I told myself, "this might be the day you get better, so hold on." Ten weeks later, I was free of the chains of prescription drugs and cocaine. I have not done hard drugs in ten years, and I have zero desire to ever go back to that life. I am free and will never again be enslaved. I still drink like a fish and deemed alcohol my truest friend and embraced it, as I begin to face my inner demons of childhood.

After detoxing, the first thing I did was to reach out to my stepfather, under the guise of just seeing how he was doing, to say "hello" etc., but the real reason was to lure him to Florida, and to personally confront him for what he did, and denied doing to both me and Brandon. We wanted to try to understand why neither of our parents ever called the police, or reported the crime of sexual abuse and assault on a minor. He is not a registered sex offender to this day.

After a week of sending emails, Gene contacted me. He was happy to hear from me. He was living in the Philippines, with a girlfriend who had an 8-year-old son. My heart sank, knowing that he was living with a child who might have suffered the same as I had. I knew that I had to find a way to get him to Florida. I told Gene about my hauling business and the good money I was making. I told him I would fly him to Florida and put him to work. He could stay with me for six months and save up a bunch of money and take it back to the Philippines. He was really excited, and agreed to come to Florida as soon as possible. I immediately booked him a flight, arriving fifteen days later. He thought he was coming for a job that didn't even exist. The trap is set.

At that time, I had not talked to my cousin Brandon since we were children. I decided that I needed to track him down to apprise him of the situation. It took less than a day to contact him. I told him that I had something important to tell him. He knew exactly what I was going to say. Brandon said he always knew in his heart that Gene had done the same thing to others. I told Brandon that it wasn't our fault. Brandon asked me what happened to me, and I told him the story of what Gene had done, and that I had "ran, yelled and told." Nothing happened as a result.

Then Brandon told me his story. He barely began before he started to break down and cry. I tried to hold myself together, listening to the things that had happened to him, and realized that I got off very lucky. It could have been much worse for me. After he finished, I told him that I had reached out to Gene, and lured him to Florida. The plane ticket was booked. He will be here in fifteen days. Brandon was jubilant. He said that no one had ever stood up for him. He felt alone. He even called me a hero. I didn't feel like one. I just knew that once, I was a scared kid, but now, I was an adult and now I can protect myself. I can stand up for myself, and I can face my fears, and this was one of my biggest fears and I needed to confront Gene, once and for all. Brandon and I talked for several days. He was under house arrest, so he could not come to Florida. The plan was for both of us to confront Gene. That wasn't going to happen.

That was not a deal-breaker for me. I had already shared my story with a lot of my friends. I had totally released any shame I held regarding the incident. It wasn't my fault. During that week, Brandon and I talked often, and he told me that in Oregon, when he was eighteen, he made a report to the police about what had happened. No one ever responded to the complaint. Gene molested Brandon in the states of California and Oregon. Gene molested me in Hawaii. The original plan was just to lure Gene to Florida and have both if us take him out to the swamps and just get rid of him. **Yes, to kill him**.

Because Brandon could not be here for the meeting, I had to think of a different way to bring retribution to this bastard. I wired my truck to record audio, and bought a camcorder to record video. I found a family picture that had Brandon and me in it and I blacked out all the faces in the picture except for Brandon's and mine. I was going to show that picture to Gene when I confronted him.

When Brandon told me that he filed a report in Oregon, I thought it was a good idea that we reach out to the police there to see what was going on with the case, and to tell them what we were planning. There is also other law enforcement that was contacted, but everybody we contacted told us that this was not a good idea. They all told me not to do it, and that we may be getting ourselves into more trouble than it is worth because if we hurt Gene, we will be going to jail.

I am pretty sure that the police had a feeling that we were going to kill Gene. I didn't care. I'd do the time just to fuck his ass up. That being said, there was a little bit of good news. The police in Portland pulled up Brandon's file, and apparently, the original investigators of Brandon's case had retired shortly after getting the case, and the file had just been sitting in a box and nobody really looked into it. They apologized. There were new investigators for the case, and they were appreciative that we reached out. They told us there was nothing they could do unless Gene was in Oregon, and had a record of being a criminal IN OREGON, or had a warrant for his arrest for some other crime. They said if we could get him to Oregon, they would arrest him, and then they would question him and get him to admit what he did to us.

We now had a better game plan. Gene's Florida arrival was four days away.

The day Gene arrived, I met him at the airport in my work truck. The person I met was a recognizable, yet visibly aged, version of the Gene I previously knew. I gave him a hug, and asked him how he was doing, He expressed his appreciation for giving him a job and a place to stay, and said how impressed he was with my success. We got his bags, and returned to my work truck. I told him "this is the truck you're going to be driving while you're here." He was really excited. I told him "hey man let's get some pictures of you in front of this truck so we can send them back to your girlfriend in Philippines." I wanted to make sure I got some new fresh pictures of his face because I had plans to post them everywhere, to warn people about this man. We got inside the truck and started to drive to where he thought was going to be my house, but I had plans to take him somewhere else.

REWIND THREE HOURS

Three hours before I went to the airport to pick up Gene, one of my friends called me and said, "Hey, I want you to come here on your way. A lot of my friends knew I was going to confront my stepfather about molesting me. When I got to my buddy's house, he told me to sit down and walked to the back of the apartment. He came out of the back room with a 9-millimeter handgun, and gently placed it on the table, as if it was explosive. He then equally gently placed a fully-loaded clip on the table, beside the gun, and said, "All I want you to do is, when you're finished, to make sure that nobody will ever find it. Throw it in the swamp." I held that gun in my hand, and I did not get a good feeling. It wasn't the premonition of death that happens in the movies. It just didn't feel right. I handed the gun back to him and I told him that I really needed to do this in a positive way, so that I can get a positive outcome. I'm not here to ruin my life. I just want a better life. Back to the airport...

I now have Gene in the truck. My plan is to drive him to the police station. That seemed like the safest place for me to confront a child molester and a rapist. We left at the airport, and got on Highway 275, about a 25-minute drive to the police station. On the way, we talked about what he had been doing in life since the last time I had seen him. He said he was homeless for quite a while and was doing a lot of criminal stuff: breaking into places and stealing, just to get by. I didn't feel at all guilty for being really happy to hear that he had been suffering for so many years. At one point, he tried to tell me that because he was still married to my mother when she passed away, that there is some money for him. I just kept my composure, although I really just wanted to punch this guy right in the fucking face.

When we pulled up to the police station, Gene didn't notice that it was a police station. He thought we were at a restaurant. He asked if he could put his luggage inside the front of the truck. I saw this as a great opportunity to get my camcorder ready. He put his first bag into the truck, and before he could pull out the second bag, I handed him the school picture of Brandon and me. I said, "Hey, do you recognize anybody in this picture?" At this point, I turned on the camcorder, and I pointed it directly at his face.

He said, "Hey, where did you get this?" I said, "Do you recognize the two kids in the picture?" Yes," he said. I asked him point blank, "Why did you molest us?" The look on his face was priceless. He was in complete shock. He said, "There's no job here, is there? You lured me here for this? Where am I going to go? I have no money. I'm going to be homeless." I told him that would be a small price to pay for the things that he had done. He grabbed his bags and started walking through the parking lot toward the sidewalk.

I was still recording, and I noticed that many people were coming in and out of the jail. I screamed "That man is a child molester and a rapist!" Gene stopped walking and turned to look at me, and the other people who were now staring directly at him. I yelled to Gene, "Let's go inside the jail, so we can talk to the police about what you did. We can clear it all up today." All he had to do is admit what he did to Brandon and me. He turned and began to walk away. I followed, continuing to record. I kept questioning him. He turned and started to talk to me. I continued recording. He denied that he did anything to either Brandon or to me. He claimed that it was Brandon's stepfather who had raped him. I asked him how he knew that to be true, and if that was the case, why he didn't report it to the police. Gene did not have answers to any of my questions, which was even more apparent after watching the video. His guilt is definitive. He didn't have to admit it. His expression spoke volumes. After about thirteen minutes of questioning and filming, there was not much more I could do or say.

I turned around and I walked into the police station, and approached the woman at the desk. I explained to her the story about my stepfather, and I told her that he had threatened me for questioning him for molesting me as a child. I explained that I had just picked him up from at airport, and told her about my plan. I told her that I was afraid that he was going to show up at my home. I asked her if there was anything that they could do. She told me no, unless he has committed a crime, or threatened me with a weapon. She told me to just go home, and if he showed up there, to call the police.

I left the station and got into my truck. As I left the parking lot, I saw him walking down the sidewalk with his baggage. He was stranded. Two days later, I got word that Gene had arrived back in Oregon. His brother and mother had bought him a plane ticket, and he was staying at his mother's house. I contacted detectives in Portland, and told them that Gene was there, and gave them the address. They thanked me for the information, and promised to keep me up to date. Within twenty-four hours, Brandon called me and said the detectives had contacted him and told him that they were on the way to pick up Gene. While still on the phone with Brandon, my Call Waiting alerted me. It was an Oregon number. I told Brandon that I would call him back. It was the detective. They told me they had picked up Gene, and they were going to question him, and try to get him to admit what he did to us. I thanked them, and then called Brandon back.

I told Brandon that they had him in cuffs and were questioning him at the station. We were overjoyed. It was like we won the lottery. Fifteen years after the fact, we were facing our molester, and he would now have to answer for the crimes that he committed. It was a beautiful feeling. We felt like we were on top of the world. It felt like justice was finally being served. That day, I grew a little stronger, because I faced the monster in the closet. It no longer scared me. That happy feeling would be short-lived.

Within the next twenty-four hours, the detectives called us back, and told us that Gene was going to be arrested, but not for what he did to us. He was arrested on other unrelated charges. They could not get him to admit that he molested or raped Brandon and me, but that it was apparent that he was not telling the truth. They said if they had more time to question him, that they were sure they could get him to admit it. I said, "So question him some more!" The detective explained that even if he admitted everything, the statue of limitations had expired, and that by law, there was nothing they could do.

It felt like someone came and took all the lottery money away; that justice was just a fairy-tale concept. Brandon and I wondered how there could be a time limitation on such a terrible crime. We were happy that he was in jail, and that his life was inconvenienced, but it wasn't going to stop him from touching another child. Eventually, he bonded out, and moved back to the Philippines. His girlfriend left him. He then married a woman with an 11-year-old daughter. I have reached out countless times through email, Facebook, and other social media platforms, to try to expose Gene for what he is, in an attempt to educate every person in this man's world that he is potentially dangerous to children. Unfortunately, it seemed that nobody cared or listened. Once again, I am experiencing how the loved ones of the molester protect them, instead of demanding justice for the molested child.

Over the next decade, from the ages of thirty-one years to forty-one, I did a tremendous amount of self-improvement. I learned to forgive my stepfather. I learned to forgive my biological father. I learned to forgive my mother for things I never thought I would be able to forgive. The more I held other people hostage for what had happened to me, and what they did or didn't do to me, the more I found that I was actually holding myself hostage. I created my own personal prison. It eventually became my place of comfort. That's where people like me were supposed to live, and the self-abuse paled in comparison to my childhood abuse. I realized that my abusers were ruling my life, and were winning, because they destroyed me. For a long time, I actually believed that was normal.

I've done a tremendous amount of personal development, which has empowered me to overcome this particular life event, and the many other instances of abuse that are still untold. The best thing to come of my development is that I was able to forgive myself for self-abuse, and began to love my previously unlovable self. Doing so has completely changed my life, and my entire way of living. It transformed my life from simply surviving to THRIVING. Life is a beautiful blessing, even considering all the pain and agony I have experienced.

I was made a survivor
Sharon Gulley

I think back now and again to the so many horrible
and tragic circumstances I found myself in time and
time again with the man I married and how I was so
young and innocent compared to him and yes even
now sometimes I cry; Maybe because it reminds me
that I was made a survivor. I was only 15 then and he
was 26 and he had two children of his own from a
previous marriage and I knew nothing about life and
to make matters worse I ended up being a child my
mother all of a sudden decided she did not want any
more. Even unto this day I have never figured out
what I done to deserve her self-devotion of making
sure I did not get to finish school or grow up safely at
home. She left and stayed gone for a month, and then
came home to let me know I no longer had a home. I
was sent away to her best friend that, at that time,
lived in Texas. I knew Marty very well for she had
always been a part of our lives growing up but I
never expected mother would give me away to her. I
was a good girl, I worked an after school part-time job
as a dish washer at a local eatery and went to school,
helped to keep the house clean, done dishes after
supper, help cook supper, wash clothes and anything
my mother needed me to do. It very deeply broke my
heart that painful day I flew out of the Jacksonville,
Florida's airport to Houston, Texas, to a world I knew

nothing about, but even as I boarded the plane, I never let her see me cry. I never asked why nor did I do anything except tell my brother and sister that I loved them so and that I would see them again someday soon. On the flight to Texas, I kept recalling the look on my father's face that day, in that moment when I looked back at him before getting into the car, I guess I was somehow hoping he would not let her send me away but he just hung his head low. I arrived in Texas within a couple of hours and it was nice to see the face of someone who really loved me and was happy to see me. It was comforting after that emotional day for it meant everything to me at that moment when I felt more alone than I ever knew a person could feel and a love and respect grew that day between us that lasted until the day she passed away in 2013. My heart still grieves for the only mother I really ever had throughout my whole life.

I don't think her children ever really understood why I had such a deep gratitude or love for her or our spiritual connection in this life, but we knew. I loved her deeply and still do even unto today. She saved my life. Just within that one moment in time, she gave me the strength of character needed to survive the horrible things that were yet to touch my life, something that I had no clue that was yet to come or how devastatingly it would change my whole world or how I would view life ever again. She had a fighting side to her that I admired and she wouldn't let anyone mistreat her for she would come right back at you. I thought she is what I want to be, never afraid of life or what may come. I guess I took that and made it a part of me and it has helped me so many times. I stayed in Texas with her for about a week or so and I told her I needed to go home, that my sister had brain cancer, and that I did not want her to die without me being by her side, if she passed away. I never told her what mother had said to me or that she never wanted me to ever come back home again, and I wasn't sure what mother said to Marty over the phone that day and we never really talked about it until many years later. I came to her one afternoon and told her I was going home and I left, and went home. When I arrived back home the look on mother's face was priceless, it told me all I would ever need to know; she did not love nor want me and I was okay with that if that was how it had to be, but I was going to see my sister and brother one way or another. I spent a couple of days home with them and answering their questions the best that I could without dragging them into the painful truth. It did not take long though before she threatened me that if I did not leave and go back to Texas that she would have the state to take me away. The next door neighbor heard everything she was saying to me. Later that evening I took a walk down to the small, beach side park. It was in close walking distance from our home, a quiet place where I would go to think in times that I needed to. The neighbor saw me sitting there and crying, so he stopped and asked if I was okay. Yes, I replied. I guess you heard all of that, I asked? Yeah, sometimes it can be hard to deal with parents, he replied. We talked for almost an hour before he drove away and I headed back home to pack up my things to leave but I wasn't going back to Texas and I had no clue where I was going to go but I knew I had to leave.

I finally decided I would hide out in the woods around the hospital for the week of my sister's surgery so I could be close to her. They removed the tumor from her brain and surgery went very well. The doctors done chemo and radiation treatments on her and she went home a week later. I stopped back by the house to see her and tell her I loved her, and was proud of her for doing so well with surgery and everything just to cheer her up and mother was standing outside doing laundry in one of those old wringer roll washers and I offered to help and she walked away. I finished the laundry for her and hung it. When I came back around to the front of the house, I seen her talking to the neighbor man and it looked like a serious conversation. I walked on over anyways to let her know it was done. To my surprise she said, thank you and walked away. By the way I said, what is your name? If we are going to be talking so often it might be nice to know each other's name, you think, I asked? He laughed and said yes. We told each other our names and he asked if I was busy later and I told him I had to leave that I had worn out my welcome and should be going. No don't be in such a hurry, he said. I don't think your mother would say anything to you about sticking around one more night. How would you know that? I asked. Well just tell me if you will be around later or not, I have to go unload this boat, dad is waiting on me at the dock, he replied. Yes I guess so, I'll be somewhere around here, but you never said what for, I replied. Would like to talk to you about something, he said. Okay, I questioningly replied. See you in a little while, he said as he walked away. Okay bye, I replied.

I went inside to visit with my brother and sister for a while and try to talk to mother, but she was cooking and folding clothes. I offered to help but she refused it, so I started packing up my bag and I gave all my things to my sister and told her they belonged to her now. I gave my famous marbles I won so many games with in elementary school to my brother and he was as happy as a lark. I picked up my bag to go and he ran to me and hugged me and I told them I loved them and left before the tears started to run down my face. I had just gotten out the driveway when our neighbor showed up. Where you going? He asked. Headed out I guess, I replied. To where? He asked. I don't know but can't be here, I said.

Come on in, I want to talk to you for a moment, He said. He lived in a small camper that was even too small for him and his children, but I made my way in and sat down at his table. Do you want something to drink? He asked. No I am fine thank you, I replied. What did you want to talk to me about? I asked. Well this may sound strange but I was thinking we could help each other out, He replied. How is that? I asked. Well I work all day and mother is getting to old to chase the babies all day and I need someone to help take care of them while I work, He said. You need a baby sitter? I asked. Yeah kind of, He replied. Well I don't live around here anymore so I don't know how I could be of help, I answered him back. Well I was thinking we would get married, He said. My eyes almost popped out of my head. Married? I said. Yeah, He said. It gives you a home off the streets and it gives my kids someone who will take good care of them while I work. I see how you are with your brother and sister and I think you would be great for the kids, He replied. I am only 15 and I am not old enough to get married, I said. I don't know anything about being married either, I said. He laughed and said it isn't that big of a deal. You are helping me and I am helping you, He said still laughing. I'm still not old enough to get married, I replied. Well that was why I was talking to your mother about you and she said she would sign the papers if you wanted to do this and that if you chose not to that she was going to call the state to take you away from here and I don't want to see that happen to you, He said calmly and ever so seemingly concerned. Really, I asked. She really told you she was going to call the state on me if I didn't marry you, I asked? Yes, that was what was told to me, He replied. Okay, I'll do it if it means we can live right here next to her, I replied. Okay, I will tell her it is a go, He said. No, I will tell her for I want to look her in the face when I tell her this, I said. Don't go over there and start no trouble now, He replied. I'm not going to start no trouble, I said. I just want to hear it from her, that's all, I said. I walked out of the camper and straight over to her in the yard where she waiting to see what my answer would be. Is it true? I asked. Is what true? She asked. Is it true that you would sign papers for your under aged daughter to marry a man twice plus her age? I asked. At least he will take care of you and take you off the streets, she said.

You put me on the streets mother, I said with tears in my eyes. I never wanted to leave home this way and you know it, I tearfully replied. Look I'm not going through this with you, you either marry him or go back to Texas and if not then the state will take you, she firmly said. Okay momma, if that is how you feel then I guess I have no choice. You can go back to Marty, she said. It's not Marty's job to raise your children and I am not going to do her that way. I will make it one way or the other somehow. I don't even know this man, but he does seem to be more concerned for my safety than you do, I said as I walked away. The very next morning we were in Alabama with license signed and I was a teenaged bride with two of his own children and one that was his ex's child, making three children in total. I thought about it all the way back home to Florida and how I would just be happy about being near my sister and brother. I would stay married to this man until I turned of age and I would then be free, but it did not work out as planned. We moved to Texas within the next two weeks right after his ex-wife came and got the children when she found out he remarried. I could not stay behind in the camper for I had no way to support myself and that wasn't the deal for my freedom, even if the kids were gone. I cried half the way there. His father sent him ahead to build a commercial blue crabbing business along the coast of Texas as he was finishing things up in Florida. Once again I had to say good bye to my home, family and friends, the only things I had ever known.

Life wasn't all I had expected it should be and I became a wife in every way and I had such a hard time adjusting to doing things I was not ready to commit to doing and when I wouldn't, the beatings took its place and sometimes that followed as well. I would cry and pray for the day I would be free from this man and all the hurtful things that he done to me. This went on for years and he had one child right after another during this so called marriage with other women and slept with whom and what he wanted, including me until I began to fight back. I took some very violent beatings and fought just as hard as I could, but there were times no matter how tough I thought I was, I lost in the end.

Self-pride and self-worth was a struggle for me every day as I would have to go out that door to work and pay for our place to live, buy food and wash his clothes and sometimes his brother's clothes as well at laundry mats. I would pile the makeup on to cover up the scars and bruises left on me just so I wouldn't lose my job. Neighbors would hear him beating me and see me stagger with concussions to work every other day but they would not come near me unless he was gone. Until one day I met a man they called Red and he brought it straight to him at our front door and threatened to beat the mess out of him if he didn't stop hitting me. That night was the worst night of my life for he left and didn't come home until 1am in the morning drunk and with three other people. There was a woman with him and two men. He came in and began to talk to me like I was garbage and I told him I was too tired from working all day to hear it and that set him off the wrong way. He slammed my head into the wall and started hitting me and I fought back but he hurt me so bad this time, all I could do was crawl to the bedroom away from everyone. He came into the room and took the mattress off the bed and laid it in the living room floor and slept in there with the woman he brought home. He told the two men there that if they wanted some to go and get it from me for he didn't care one way or the other, I was nothing but a slut anyway. I managed out of fear to pull myself up and slide the dresser in front of the door and lay on the floor in front of it for the rest of the night. I could hear him having sex with her and the men finally left because I wouldn't open the door or speak to them. I heard one of them tell him, I think you killed her man. I doubt it, she is just mad as hell right now. She will be alright in the morning, he replied. When they were done having sex, they left in the car. The next morning came and my eyes were swollen shut, my ribs were black and blue, and my mouth was in a terrible mess, teeth and all were lose. I was still spitting up blood and it was all I could do to breathe so I just laid there. About an hour later I heard someone at my window outside. Hey lady, are you okay? Can you hear me? I didn't say anything at first but then he said. They are all gone, your safe now, you can come out. Are you okay? He asked again. I slowly pulled myself up and hobbled over to the window and there stood a man I had never seen before.

He wasn't a real big man but he seemed so sweet and concerned. He lived in the home in front of ours. I am okay, thank you for asking, I said. You look hurt really bad lady do you want me to call an ambulance? He asked. No thank you, I said. I have been here before, it will be okay in a little while, I just need some coffee, I replied. I will go make some, He said. No that is okay, I have some here, I replied. Please let me help you, He said. It would be my pleasure. Thank you so much, I said. What is your name,? He asked me. Sharon, Sharon that is my name, I said. My name is Dave, Sharon and I am going to get you some coffee, I will be right back, He said. I couldn't pull the dresser away from the door because I was hurt to bad so he called a couple of friends and they pushed the door open from the outside and helped me out of the bedroom to the dining room chairs. I noticed Dave was once wounded his self and moved slowly when he walked but I never asked anything at the time. He came right on in and handed me a hot cup of coffee just like he said he would. I kept looking at the mattress on the floor and I started to cry. It wasn't because he had slept with her it was the thoughts of what could have happened that night. Dave and his friends took me out of the house and over to theirs and helped me to clean my face up and access the damage done to my teeth and mouth. By then the coffee had cooled down enough that I could sip it through a straw. I realized how bad I was hurt and went to the hospital anyway. I was there for 3 days while recovering. I never pressed charges for being in fear that he might retaliate and I couldn't take another beating like that, so I went back home and showered, cleaned up the place. He did not come home for a week after I got out of the hospital, but in those quite days, I met some of the most wonderful people I have ever known. They were true friends to me and even though I haven't seen them in years, I will love them always for their friendship and kindness to a young girl, they did not even know. In the state we were in there was a law that stated that if a spouse was under age, the oldest spouse was there guardian as well as their spouse and reporting this kind of violence was just something most women wouldn't do. I waited out my time and when I turned of age and yes even bore him a son during this time, I took my child and I left for good.

The emotional turmoil had ripped my life apart in so many ways, that even now a simple raise of the voice causes me to get fighting mad. I am a much bigger and stronger woman now than I ever was back then and fear for me now holds no meaning. I will never again tolerate any kind of abuse no matter what it is and believe it or not I am now my mother's caretaker, she has Alzheimer's and Dementia. Dad and sister has passed away, cancer claimed her life at the young age of 34 and Dad's as well. My brother lives up north and we talk from time to time but I take care of mother every day and have for 6 years now. Even with all I went through I could never turn my back on her for I still love her anyways. I still break down and cry sometimes for all the childhood lost and for the hugs I longed for when I felt afraid, alone and lost, but there is one thing I do know from the bottom of my heart, loving your-self and believing in yourself can heal all. Against all odds I am an Author, photographer, artist, creator, story teller, caretaker, wife, mother, sister, grandmother, cancer survivor and last now but never least, a domestic violence survivor to date. Believe in yourself, be strong and never ever except defeat for starting over at any time or age is never too late.

Sharon Gulley

Courtney Killian

I don't know how I knew it was him. I just knew. I never saw a picture of him while we were dating, but as I stared into the cold, unfeeling eyes of that mugshot, somehow I knew that my toxic ex-boyfriend had been thrown in jail for impersonating a police officer as an excuse to touch a woman's butt.

Being 15 is tough already. Throw in a 20-year-old boyfriend, and suddenly life at 15 just becomes a whole lot tougher. Make that boyfriend a very toxic person, and life becomes even tougher.

I met this man on a teen forum online. He seemed like a sweet guy, and it wasn't long before I gave him my number. I thought it was odd that he didn't offer his in exchange and that he didn't text me right after he got my number, but I didn't think much of it. Maybe he noticed my age or something, and that's why he didn't. He lost interest when he saw that I was 15. That had to be it.

For the next several days, I got a call from a private number. I thought maybe I would answer it, but my parents were always around and I didn't want them to know that I answered just anyone who called. Well, one day they were gone, and that private number called. I answered it. It was him. The man I had met on the teen forum.

Right away he started asking these weird questions, like exactly where I was located. I told him, and then the questions got even weirder. I got questions like, "Have you ever been constipated? I bet you are now."

I wasn't sure why he was asking these questions. I had never been asked before, but I kept answering them, thinking maybe he knew something I didn't. Yeah. I was a little naïve.

He also told me he was an FBI agent. I should have seen that as a red flag, but being the naïve person I was, I thought that was amazing and told him that it would be awesome if he could be transferred here and he could protect me. Did I mention he was 20? The minimum age for being an FBI agent is 23, and everyone except for me knew it.

Just two days after we talked on the phone, he asked me to be his girlfriend. I automatically said yes. That's when things got extremely worrisome. He wanted to see a nude picture of me. I told him that goes against everything I believe in, and he shouldn't be asking for things like that. He told me that if I didn't, he would come to Texas, find me, and beat me to death. I get the feeling that that's the reason he wanted to know exactly where I lived.

Fearing for my life, I sent the picture to the number he provided. Whether or not it was his actual phone, I still don't know. I never asked because naturally, I thought it was. Well, he saw the picture, and he proceeded to point out every flaw my body has. "You're too fat. You need to lose weight. You need to get rid of the glasses. You look too young. You will never be good enough."

This happened every single night of the relationship. I couldn't believe he would say this to me. My boyfriend would intentionally leave me in tears every single night that I was with him. He also made me stay up all night or at least most of the night to talk to him. Knowing me, even if I had thought to just hang up, I wouldn't have because I like to think I'm extremely loyal.

Really, red flags were all around this relationships. Many happened before the relationship actually became official, but the first one that appeared after he asked me to be his girlfriend appeared about five minutes later. He told me he loved me. I had just been stung in an earlier relationship, so I knew I wasn't going to say it right away. I didn't want to make the same mistake again. Well... At least that's what I thought. He made me say it. I had to practically force it out. I had a hard time with it. I was on the phone all night with him and even when my alarm went off, he made me say it before I got off the phone to get ready for school. Yeah. It was a school night that I stayed up all night on the phone with him.

This happened many, many nights. The same thing over and over again. The next night that I really remember was at my friend's birthday party. He insisted that we text while I was there, and that was fine. Well, then he called, and I ignored the call because I was spending time with my friends. Then he called again. And again. Then he sent me a text. "Don't you dare ignore my call again because I will find you tonight. I have a belt ready." I answered the next time and missed the rest of the party.

Everyone knew he was no good except for me. He proposed to me a week in the relationship and I said yes. I considered it an official engagement at the time, but now I don't because I never saw him in person. I never even saw his picture while we were dating, which I now think of as another red flag.

Everyone told me, "You need to leave him. He's no good. You don't need to talk to him anymore." I had many arguments with my parents about him. He told me we could forget about them.

He kept telling me how amazing sex could be. He told me what I could and could not do online. He told me what I could and could not wear out in public. He made the decision or not as to whether I could wear anything in bed. He also told me that I wouldn't look good no matter what I was in, if anything, and if I didn't change that, he would beat me to death.

There was a point where my self-esteem was nonexistent, and I was in such a deep depression that I knew I couldn't take the relationship any more. It was hard, but I eventually broke up with him.

The thing is, I didn't realize how toxic my situation was until about a year after I left him. I couldn't believe I had missed all those red flags. Then I got angry. I got angry at myself. I got angry at him. I couldn't believe he treated me that way, and I couldn't believe I had let him treat me that way. I started thinking about how he talked about sex all the time, and so I got curious... I started watching pornography and eventually it became the only way I could curb my anger enough to be around people and not completely snap. I couldn't go a single day without it or I would not be pleasant to be around at all.

This kept going for three long years. It's safe to say that I didn't have many friends at this point in time. I hated myself and everyone around me.

After sitting on this anger for about three years, I woke up in the middle of the night one night and got this idea for this book. I thought, "That's a stupid idea. Nobody is going to read that. Whoever heard of a murder mystery when the murderer is the narrator, anyway?" I fought that for an hour, but it wouldn't go away, and I couldn't go back to sleep. I eventually gave up, turned my laptop on, and wrote it... I wrote 6,000 words that first night.

Miracles happen... I was less angry the next day. I kept writing the book, and I became less and less angry every single time. Eventually, I was the happy person I used to be again. I still had very little self-esteem, but I could actually be pleasant around people and I actually enjoyed interactions.

I've been in several toxic relationships since this one I wrote about. Publishing a book has been a dream of mine since I was seven years old. I was told I would never do it. Well, I proved all of my abusers wrong.

I believed lies for way too long. I believed what they told me. Now, I believe myself to be the imperfect work in progress, yet beautiful masterpiece that has been through the mud and cleaned herself off.

I mentioned that this man was arrested for impersonating a police officer at the beginning. I feel like I finally got my closure of all toxic relationships from just that one small victory and I can finally move on with my life.

I'm not perfect. I still struggle. I've been suicidal. I still battle depression and anxiety. But I am also wonderful. I am beautiful. I have kicked the pornography addiction. I love myself. My self-esteem is at an all-time high and I love it.

I am not only surviving after being through this terrible event, but I am thriving. I have the incredible opportunity to meet all sorts of people while doing author signings and tell my story. My goal is to help just one person through telling my story. I have gotten to where I will tell people with no hesitation, and I want as many people as possible to hear it.

I'm living my life the way I want to live it now. I'm done with playing by someone else's rules. It's my life, and I'm thriving. Nobody is going to control me ever again.

"Tell your heart to beat again. Close your eyes and breathe it in. Let the shadows fall away. Step into the light of grace. Yesterday's a closing door. You don't live there anymore. Say goodbye to where you've been, and tell your heart to beat again."

-Danny Gokey

A life lived in fear – by Abigail Hope

A life lived in fear is a life half lived….. This phrase was a magnet on the door of the fridge in my family home for years. I have an almost photographic memory so it still remains clear to me to this day. The irony of this is that my mother has lived much of her life in fear. She will never admit to it and her amazing poise, her catholic faith and her co-dependency on my father will forever mask her fears.

My parents had a tumultuous and abusive relationship. Some parts I remember very clearly; yet other memories have been recounted to me by my older brother and they seem to be the most violent ones. I am not sure if I was just too little to remember or the trauma of these has helped me to forget but it would seem I don't remember the worst of it.

My parents' relationship did mellow as we grew up and as they grew older but the control and the narcissistic nature of how my father treated my mother remains to this day. One very clear and poignant feeling I always remember growing up and as a teenage girl was how badly I wanted my mum to leave her marriage. This is an unusual thing in hindsight because I truly believe children want to see their parents together and the family to be a unit. But not me…. I wanted my mother to pick up, pack up and run the fuck away. To my surprise she did one day but only for one night to the local motel and she called my dad on the phone to tell him where she was. Not the toughest stand but the actions of a very unassertive and dominated wife. If she had of never returned I would have cheered and wholeheartedly understood. She returned dutifully the next day as if nothing had happened. She was never equipped to leave and still today I wonder how on earth she would survive on her own. Yet so badly and so genuinely I wanted my mum to find the strength, the courage or the self love to leave him. To show my father that she valued herself more than the abusive marriage she had pledged herself to.

This is not the point of my story at all. I am just setting the context or perhaps trying to justify my own journey into an equally abusive and violent marriage.

Fast track yourself a few years down the track to me as a skinny teenage girl. I was sixteen years old and I lived in a small country town where football was religion and football players were gods. I had bounced around a few relationships with boys at school but nothing serious or lasting.

He was a handsome boy in a Nirvana t'shirt, drove a fast commodore and had a left step on the football field that made him dangerous. I thought that I loved him from the first time that I saw him and I will never forget the friend I was with at the time told me to stay away from him.

I was drawn to him and I knew how to play my cards right to get his attention. There were no phones or text messages or Facebook chats to let someone know you were interested in these days. You would go to the football, cheer for your crush and follow the team to the pub afterwards. There were parties, alcohol and we did lots of flirting, cute letter writing and some awkward first dates. Soon enough he was mine and I was hooked. He was my drug of choice but unfortunately I wasn't his. In fact lots of other woman were his first choice but I was too young, too naïve and too in love to see. The town that we grew up in had a serious drinking culture and he spent a lot of his time partying and drinking alcohol. He was a local football hero and I was a young, sheltered yet vivacious girl so I still to this day wonder what part of me didn't know how to run the fuck away.

I was smart and had to move away from my hometown to study at university while he couldn't be drawn away from the wondrous social life of our hometown. He was a tradesman and didn't pursue any further career or study but worked, drank copious amounts of alcohol, played football and fought at the pub on weekends with anyone that looked sideways at him or pissed him off. returned home every weekend a five hour round trip to keep the romance alive. I had a wonderful time at university and I had so many friends and memories made. Every Friday I would make the trip home to him and back to my hometown to sit in the pub and watch him drink.

He was a second generation rugby player like his father and his father was his greatest fan. A jolly man with a heart of gold but sadly a legacy he taught to his son that would serve to haunt him in later years. He was taught to solve problems with his fists. His father instilled deeply into both of the sons in the family that if someone pissed you off you fixed it with a punch or two. I am sure he intended this only to be applicable to other equally drunk males at the pub however it is a coping strategy that he adopted and used in many situations. The cracks began to appear in these years where there were lots of drunken scuffles, pushing, and shoving, forcing, yelling and general standover tactics in our relationship but always fuelled by alcohol so I came to accept this as his behaviour when he wasn't sober. But it begs the question – why a smart, attractive and vivacious young girl with a whole world of opportunity and male species at University in the city would give up every weekend to return to this relationship. I told myself it was love.

He was taught to ignore matters of the heart and communicate with ignorance and silence but to bury feelings deep inside until a drunken night or a catalyst event and he would explode with rage and all the unresolved anger would come spewing out of him. He would yell, hit things, slam doors, make threats and at the worst physically hurt me or make accusations about my behaviour or force sexual demands on me. Eventually I moved home the dutiful girlfriend to live in my hometown with him and we moved into our first home together. To this man I believed I loved and eventually married.

His life was an ongoing fight, a raging fight within himself to deal with feelings and emotions and with no coping skills it became domestic violence. Now in hindsight it feels like such a breath of relief to understand that behaviour and put a name to it. I will never justify it but I have come to understand it, call it what it is and move on from its hold over me. It actually had become a marriage fraught with fear, with control and where problems were solved with violence.

I have never had a black eye and I have rarely sported visible bruises. That is not to say that there wasn't times when he hurt me physically as there were many times that I was injured by him mostly in an alcohol fuelled rage. I have lots of memories but never seemed to have any witnesses to the violence only the injuries that he inflicted and I lied about the true cause of those.

Once at a party he torn a windscreen wiper off a car and hit me across the legs with it. These injuries were easily covered by long trousers until they had healed. Another time he tackled me to the ground on the concrete and I broke my finger in the fall, a sports injury to all my family and friends. Perhaps the worst altercation we ever had was on a beach and he threw me around like a rag doll because I threw his mobile phone into the ocean so he would stop calling his girlfriend. The following day bruises started appearing all over my body one at a time. We were attending a rock concert with friends that night and I had to get one of my friends to do my hair because I couldn't lift my hands above my head. As she did my hair she asked me about the injuries and I remember that I told her I fell off a fence. I didn't have to tell her because she already knew and we both cried as she finished my hair..... I will never forget and she told me that when I was ready to tell her the truth she was going to be there to help me. Sadly she is no longer my friend because she couldn't stand to know me anymore and the things that were happening to me without being able to help me.

Sadly I lost many friends along the journey because they knew things weren't right but didn't know how to help. Part of the violence was also the control. He would control my phone, my emails, my conversations and what I was and wasn't allowed to say to people. He deteriorated relationships with family and friends because I was no longer allowed to talk to people about anything personal. We lived on a farm and we became very isolated. Still I loved him; still I stayed and put huge amounts of energy into my marriage because I had signed up for life. I stayed with him for ten years of dating and ten years of marriage. That's more than half of my life to date! We had two beautiful children together and with each life event, each new house, each new year, each child I had renewed optimism that he would change. The control and the fear are the things that impacted on me the most. I felt like a scared bird in a cage always walking a tightrope. I feared spending money, I feared getting text messages from friends, I feared making any wrong move and that fear gave him control.

The decision to leave him was made years before I actually left and I still believed that I loved him until that time. I told my best friend that I wanted to leave him and she unknowingly organised an intervention with my parents because she was unaware of my real reasons for wanting to leave. Everyone came to see me, to stop me and convince me to stay. I had to take medication and have counselling because I was clearly a crazy wife who had flipped her lid and I was separating my family. I felt so unsupported and violated by this move that I just resigned to this being my fate after all it was for better or worse and I stayed another year.

In that year I worked to become an emotionless robot because I knew the only way I could really leave and never come back was to have no emotional ties to him so that when the time to leave arrived nothing would stop me. I was desperately unhappy, I was trapped and scared and I became a risk taker. I had a certain disregard for myself and my own life and wanted to either die or piss him off so much that he would make a public display of violence so that I had my instant leave pass and everyone would understand why I was leaving him. Sadly it never occurred to me in these years that the choice was mine and mine alone. That I did not need permission to leave from anyone but myself and that love real love looked nothing like this.

I became an agitator and I knew how to make him react. The bigger the better as far as I was concerned. I wanted him to harm or injure me as much as possible because I felt like I needed to prove to people that I was being abused. I deliberately agitated any way that I could.... spent large amounts of money. If he commented that he liked my long hair.... The next day I would cut it ultra-short to displease him. If I had agreed to arrive home by a particular time.... I would come home two hours later. I started texting my friends incessantly and letting my phone repeatedly chime so that he knew I was getting lots of messages but I would change the pin numbers and passwords to my phone so he could no longer read my messages. I changed the password to all of my email accounts to drive him crazy. I pushed and pushed the barriers because I wanted his next explosion to be public and explosive so it could be finally witnessed and people would know what was happening.

I also started to take risks because I thought that if I could accidently die then the problem would also be solved. I had developed a distinct lack of confidence or regard for myself and I would drive my car fast and I crashed my car a number of times. I would drink alcohol and swim in the home pool hoping that I may accidentally drown. I would ride my bike as fast as I could down hills and close my eyes hoping that I would fall off and break my neck. Fortunately I am still alive and well but sadly that person saw death as an alternative to leaving the relationship. How does this happen?

The final fight we ever had was public. Sadly it was in front of my sister, her husband and our children. I never wanted my children to witness this and until this time they never had seen physical violence. He was not drunk but he was wild. I had made him wild and he dragged me around by the hoody on my jumper, he locked me in a room and forced me around, he locked me in a car and tried to drive it away recklessly. This went on and on into the night until my sister threatened to call the police. I was petrified but I was free! The saddest moment in my life was my children being frightened of their father as he man handled their mother.

This moment I realised that I had been selfish and foolish. My children had become me.... That child I remembered who willed for her mother to leave her father. My children were not going to watch their mother go through this anymore and I left him. It is still to this day the single hardest thing that I have ever done. I left not because of the abuse and not because of the fear I left because of those two children. No matter what happened in life and no matter how I felt; I was not going to let those girls grow up to become like me. I was not going to let them down and have them too believe that any woman should be frightened, controlled or abused. I was not going to let them believe for one moment that this was love! I was not going to raise another generation of woman to live in fear. Not for one more day because a life lived in fear is not a life half lived...... it is in fact a life taken away, a life lost, a spirit crushed and a soul destroyed.

I was broken and I was defeated and it was the most scary and beautiful day of my life because I knew that little girl who wanted so badly for her mother to pick up, pack up and fuck off had drawn strength from that and she had become the strong woman that she needed to be to leave and no one had taught her how to do that she had to summons the strength and courage to do it for herself. It had to come from me, from within because what I hadn't realized was that I was never going to be encouraged to leave by a family who had shared the same demons for so long.

I moved in with my parents for a short while but they wanted me to have a reunion with my husband; even after I had told them selective and sorry details of the past. I so desperately wanted their support with this but they could not understand or would not understand it was too raw for them. I think they saw in my relationship a reflection of themselves or perhaps it was guilt and to accept my decision was too confronting to them. I had to find that support in friends and I did. I had many supporters who were my stronghold through this storm. It took time and courage and there isn't a day my heart doesn't ache for the experience and the pain but it has faded. I am calm and I am strong and totally resolute that I will never allow myself to be treated or mistreated by anyone again.

When I had left and he could no longer control me he tried to control those who were closest to me with his tales of woe. The loving and lonely husband and father to the selfish and crazy wife who had left him devastated. But that is when I stopped telling my story and I stopped trying to justify my actions because I had come to realize that I was endlessly seeking approval to leave. I wanted clear cut visible reasons to exit my marriage and what I didn't understand until now is that approval from another person didn't matter. The one and only person qualified to make that decision was me and me alone. Somewhere in the crazy and mixed up thing that I called love I had lost sight of what love actually was. Not love for another person, self-love, true and unconditional self-love. I had forgotten how to love myself and how to care for myself first. The love that you deserve the most is your own and I have come to truly believe that because without it how can we even know how to love another. How can we teach our children to love if we cannot show them first that we love ourselves? If my own mum knew how to truly love herself then she could have shown me. This is now my commitment to me and my girls to show and teach them of the greatest love for one's self that you can have. If they can love themselves then they will in turn never have this same fate.

Violence against woman is portrayed in the media as purple bashed faces under darkened sunglasses. However violence against woman takes many forms some more subtle and some more inconspicuous but the underlying motivation is always the same. The purpose is to control a person's behavior and to inflict fear on the woman when she doesn't play to suit. It isn't always a visible thing to outsiders but the damage and the emotional scars are just as hideous as the visible ones.

The problem with this image is that as a woman in an abusive and violent relationship I felt that if the evidence wasn't readily visible the crime could not be confirmed. But no one has the right to instill any kind of fear or threat to another person. That in itself is enough reason to leave. So if you are in a relationship where you have fear of any kind that is enough for you to leave. Don't look for the bruises, don't agitate for a response, don't devalue yourself because of the actions of another and don't try to seek approval from others as to why you should leave. Just leave.

There is a saying that resounds with me now from the wizard of Oz; when Dorothy wants to leave Oz and return home to Kansas and the good witch says to her "You always had the power my dear, you just had to learn it for yourself" and she taps together the heels of the red shoes she has been wearing from the start and returns home.... that is exactly how I feel.

I always had the power I just hadn't been shown how to use it so I had to learn it for myself. That was a long and difficult journey but it has brought me to a place or strength and growth. This story is not one I tell many people and it's difficult to tell without a rush of tears and emotion but if it can help you to find that power my dear it's a story worth sharing!

Kim's Journey

Who am I to write this? When someone asks who I am, I often reply that I am love incarnate and infinite possibility. I have learned this to be true. Not just of me but of all beings on this planet. But I'm sure you are more interested in a a definition that you can sink your brain into. I am a 50 year old person that has lived a lot of life. I have helped many, many along the way to realize their dreams and to truly realize love. I am currently a life coach living in Los Angeles, California. When approached to write this chapter about some of the trials of my life that surround domestic violence, I was honored.

Before I even knew the name of the book that would be published, I started to write. As I wrote, one of the things that came forward to me was my own ability to be resilient. Having worked with so many beautiful souls, it also came to me, just how resilient we can all be. The infinite potential of each one of us. The journeys that we take in order to progress into various state of awareness of love, faith and hope. I understand what it is like to suffer greatly. I believe that we all do. I have attempted to express some of that suffering in the following pages. Not so that anyone could feel for me but so others could find a commonality. Particularly those that still suffer so that they may know that there is hope for their suffering to end. Each life is a winding tale with many intricacies. Because of this I have chosen to wind around a bit with my fashion of writing here. Be assured though, that things will tie together nicely in the end. As has my life. As I hope yours will.

The first memory I had until a few years ago was of my mother being beaten by her first husband. I was three years old. It was the 1960's and women had little to no recourse at that time. When he left, my mother simply worked to take care of my sister and I, and there was no counseling for children that had been victims of domestic violence. Though I had not been beaten by him, my mother sometimes lashed out at me. She was beside herself and there was very little help for her. She was seen as a bad woman. She was treated by society as if she was the one that had done something wrong. She did not and was not wrong. She survived the only way she knew how, by becoming tough and not allowing any sort of vulnerability to creep in. I write this because the essence of this is what set the stage for what I grew up to endure and become. My name is Kim and this is my story.

Today, I am not at all afraid of being vulnerable. I am not afraid to love, but it took me many years and lots of healing, looking under every rock possible to find the way to my own heart. I always knew it was there but didn't quite know how to find it. Some would brand me a victim, some would brand me a perpetrator. Am I both or neither? I feel I am neither.

At the age of 12 or 13 I began to use drugs. Mostly marijuana and alcohol. Up until that time I was a straight-A student who always did my best to stay out of any sort of trouble, but I didn't feel loved at all. I did everything in my power to avoid the emotional outbursts and occasional beatings, but I grew tired. My mother did not seem to see me or hear me, and my step father simply went along for the ride. I remember speaking to a family friend years later that told me she had never seen a child more starved for affection. So I began to escape.

I never built up an addiction to any drug so I thought I was fine. It was just for recreation. Then came the sex. My first time was fine, it was with a boy my age when I was 13. I wanted to be held and loved. I thought that if I was pretty enough and smart enough, a boy would come along and love me, and give me the affection that I longed for. So, I did everything that I could to make myself desirable to the opposite sex. I slept with them on a whim. I told myself that I was fine. There was nothing wrong with what I was doing. After all, I only slept with the good ones. Those that treated me with affection. Until one day, when my mother was having another outburst after having found out what I was doing again, I ran away. I hung out with the druggy kids because they were the only ones who seemed to embrace me. I needed a place to go so I found boys that allowed me to crash with them for a price. My body.

I ran away from home four times between the ages of 13 and 15, once staying gone for six months. My parents did try to put me in counseling but to no avail. The first counselor simply said I was unruly and there was no hope. The second one treated me with love but she could not get me to express my pain. I was terrified to speak of what my household was really like and I thought myself tough. I was told not to talk about what went on at home for so long that I could not mentally open up to her. Each time that I was belittled and blamed and told that I was not allowed to feel angry or hurt a part of me died inside. I was literally the walking dead and I genuinely believed that this was what life was supposed to be like. I could never do anything right so why try? The only thing I knew how to do was to behave in whatever way I was taught to. I had no real feelings of being a person. I was to do what I was told, but why did something deep inside rebel? I had no idea. All I knew was that I was broken and I must have been born this way. But if I could just find someone to hold me and love me my life would be better. That would mean that I was not broken. That I deserved to be loved.

At the age of 16 my mother's best friend set me up on a blind date. I had recently broke up with a boyfriend and was being told to "get back on the horse." What I wanted to do was to spend some time with myself. I knew instinctively that it wasn't what I needed, but I didn't listen to myself. Instead I did what I was being told was in my best interest. I went on the date.

He was a couple of years older than me and shy. I liked that he was shy. It made me feel comfortable, not threatened, and he was a bit of a rebel. He had a decent job and a decent car and was able to take me out. I liked that as well. He didn't push me for sex like most guys did. Though once we did engage in sex it was very good. He was so giving. Never mind that he drank and smoked pot daily. He functioned at work and home and he was a good lover. So how could he have a problem with these substances? After dating for a year he asked me to marry him. I had graduated high school, was working two jobs and attending school at a local community college. I didn't want to get married. But he asked and I said no. I said no 3 times. But I had been home and at home my mother kept browbeating me. I worked from 5am til 4pm, and attended school from 7pm til 10pm, five days a week. I was never home and I was paying rent, but I was still expected to do the dishes when I came, do chores and spend time with my family on the weekend. I could barely breathe and I had no time to spend with friends or my boyfriend aside from weekend nights. I felt alone. I felt like no matter what I did, it was not good enough. My school work suffered because it was a matter of taking care of school work or having time to spend with someone that I felt loved me. So, I got married. I got married because I thought that he would support me in my endeavors. I did make this known to him but once married he became a tyrant.

He was jealous of everyone and everything. If we walked into a restaurant and someone looked my way, I had slept with him. His friends would come to visit and I would make food. They often complimented me and him for having such a great wife. But he saw that as me trying to flirt and get the attention of others. He became more and more controlling. Soon, he began to pick fights when I was attempting to do my schoolwork and when he knew I had to leave for work. I failed too many classes and had to drop out of school. Of course this was seen by everyone one as being my fault, especially by me. I lost job after job because my home life was in constant turmoil. My husband often got into fights with others and that landed him in jail. I used pot to escape. I just wanted to feel good, if only for a moment. And if I could just be a better wife, if I could just help my husband fix his problems, things would be OK. I loved him, and love should conquer these demons. Whenever my husband would feel like he had done something wrong with me, he would buy me things. Things we could not afford. He wanted to be the provider and have me under his thumb, but I could not see that. All I could see is a man in a great deal of pain. A man I loved and someone that I wanted to make happy.

I would tell myself that he was not abusive. He never hit me. Though when he started in on me I would try to leave and he would often pin me up against the wall and laugh at me. Pretty soon he would beg me to stay and I would. But he would start in again. It was a feeling of being trapped in more than one way. I had no money to leave and as soon as I would start to do well at a job, he would make sure that was put to a stop. I felt absolutely powerless, alone and afraid. My mother told me that I had made my bed and that I had to deal with it. There was no compassion or understanding. There never had been. I was 19 years old and had no clue or tools to navigate the world with. Yet, I was expected to do so. I had been isolated because my husband ran off my friends. He often made them feel uncomfortable. I found out later that he had even gone so far as to make sexual advances toward my best friend. She simply stopped talking to me. Like me, she felt powerless and like all advances towards her were her fault.

In the 1980's cocaine was all the rage, and we occasionally partook. Then my husband found free basing. At first, due to lack of funds, he could only partake on rare occasions. I tried it but didn't care for it. I didn't understand why someone would want a high that only lasted for a few minutes and cost so much. Thank goodness I did not have the type of brain that was easily addicted to substances. Unfortunately my husband did. He eventually lost his job where he had just got a promotion and we were to have been more financially stable. He started selling cocaine without my knowledge and when I found out the fights escalated. He did this behind my back. He would come home high and out of his mind. Until one day I decided that no matter that I had no money and really nowhere to go, I was leaving. I packed a bag and waited for him to come home. When he did, he was high on cocaine. I talked to him and told him that I had to leave. That I was sinking and that I no longer loved him. He went crazy. He blocked the door and laughed at me. He started telling me that if I left he would kill my family. The energy was intense and I was frightened for my life. He sat in front of me hammering this idea at me that he was going to kill me and my family. I bolted for the door several times but each time he caught me, twisted my arm and pull me back to the sofa. I was trapped. After a long time I finally decided to pick up the phone. I didn't call the police because my husband had told me that if I did he would tell the cocaine dealers he was working with to kill me. I called my parents and my dad picked up the phone. I pleaded with him for help but he told me to just call the police, that he could not help me. My husband ripped the phone out of the wall and grabbed me by my hair. He was laughing at me and pushed me down to the floor. I got up and went go the kitchen sink to get some water. I was sobbing. He then lunged at me with his fist. At the point where he was lunging I saw my opportunity. There was a knife on the counter. I grabbed it and stabbed for his heart. Thank goodness he moved. I ended up stabbing him in the shoulder blade.

Here was my opportunity. I made for the door once more as my husband was reeling over the pain. I made it down the stairs of our apartment building and was able to get into my car before he showed up standing in front of me. The car was old and needed work so it didn't start up right away. He proceeded to try his keys while I was trying to start it but I held down the lock while attempting to start the ignition. I was finally able to start the car but he had already unlocked the hatchback and was climbing in. I drove sporadically with him in the back of the car. I made it two miles before he was able to grab my hands on the wheel and squeeze so tight that I thought he had broken my bones. This caused me to run the car up on a telephone pole. I opened the door and began to run towards my mother's home. I was about a mile away. My husband followed me as I ran. As I made my way into a middle class neighborhood early in the evening I began to yell for help, "Help, help, he is trying to kill me." I shouted and shouted but nobody came out, turned on a light, or called the police. My cries went unanswered, and he continued to pursue me, taunting me by saying things like nobody cares whether I live or die. I did finally make it to my parent's house and my husband stopped the pursuit a block away. I was frightened but I hardly showed it. I was just happy to be away from him. I never went back.

I did my best to recover in the following months. Got a new job, found a roommate situation and thought I had put all of this behind me. I partied with my friends, dated, and was aware that my husband had moved away when he came by to tell me he was doing so and that I could finally collect my things. I had two short lived relationships. One was a college student that turned out to be addicted to methamphetamine. The other was with someone I got engaged to but that didn't work out because... he loved me too much. I didn't really know how to love yet. So I sabotaged the relationship by simply being mean to him. After my marriage I began to pride myself on how tough I was. What I didn't understand was that toughness was very weak. It was a wall I had built in order to not actually feel. It pushed everyone away from me that had the potential to show me love.

Then I met Mark. We fell for each other instantly and within 2 months we had moved in together. For the first six weeks it was blissful. He was so romantic. Then he began to change. He started to criticize everything I did. What I wore, what I cooked, even the way I walked and spoke. One night he came home and didn't seem himself at all. He appeared pale and his eyes were a bit bugged. When I asked him if he was OK, his head rolled back, then he stared into me and said; "I am not Mark." I do not remember what he said his name was but he claimed that he hated me because he actually loved me. That he was homosexual and that he had sex with men in restrooms. I didn't believe what I was hearing. I was beyond bewildered. So I asked questions and played along. The energy felt thick and real but my brain could not compute this. Was he insane? Playing some sort of a game? What was this? I stayed. And the next day I got a call from a family member telling me my mother was having emergency brain surgery. So I went to the hospital to wait to see if she would make it. She did but that meant that she had to learn to walk, talk, speak and eat all over again. I was 21 and I had almost lost my mother. I was in quite a state, trying to work and figure out what to do about my relationship, where to live and what my next move in life would be. Do I stay? Where will I go? Is my mother going to be able to live a life at all again? All I wanted was to be loved but it was not meant to be. My boyfriend refused to talk with me about my mother or anything about my life for that matter. He was closing off, going missing for long amounts of time, and I was holding on, trying to figure out what to do.

One night he came home and ignored me again. I felt frustrated and hurt. Once again I had really messed up. No matter what I did it was never good enough and everything was my fault. I should have known better. In my frustration I began to sob. He was in another room but shouted at me to shut up. I didn't want to make things worse but I could not help sobbing. I tried to do so quietly but he grew angry and before I knew it he was standing over me. I looked up at him and the first blow across my face knocked me out of nowhere. Before I knew it, he reached down, picked me up and threw me across the room. I struggled to stand but before I could, he reached down and picked me up by my throat. There I was pinned against the wall by my throat, unable to breathe, my life flashing before my eyes. Suddenly, he snapped back and let go of me. I fell to the ground in a puddle. He began to cry and apologize but I was terrified. I crawled to the bathroom mirror to look at myself and felt anger well up. I remember him looking in on me and saying "It's not that bad." That made me even more angry and I ran for the door. I had nothing with me. Not my purse, no shoes on. All I knew was that I could not be anywhere near him. He was changing again and I was in danger. I made my way next door to the establishment that I worked at. As I entered the door my co-worker took one look at me and got on the phone to the police. She was asking me what had happened when he came in and began blaming me for what he had done. He did not leave until the police put him in the back of the car. That night I made my first call to a battered women's hot line. I was given a number to a shelter and instructed to leave before he got out of jail. I did this and was welcomed into the shelter by the next day. I only spoke to him once after that. He was busy blaming me but all I wanted was to collect my belongings. I did so at an arranged time when he would be gone and with the assistance of a friend.

I spent a month at the shelter in counseling and managed to continue to work at the same place without seeing him. I had a restraining order that did not allow him to come anywhere near me. I don't know what happened at court because I opted not to go. All I wanted was to be free. I spent some time in counseling over the next year and that was somewhat helpful. I was able to consciously see that it was not my fault. I thought that was all I needed to know. That and how to spot those that would try to harm me. I do not know what was wrong with Mark, but he obviously had some serious things to work on. What I didn't understand was, so did I. Within a year I joined the army. I was 22 years old and I thought that I could help to make the world a better place. It was a good fit for me. I always wanted people to see me as the strong person I felt that I was. I always wore girly clothes, make up and never had a hair out of place. I prided myself on my appearance. But I felt like I wanted to show everyone that they had underestimated me. That I was more than some pretty face and didn't need a man to take care of me. I could do this. I was smart, strong and wanted to change the world.

I chose an occupation in the army that would challenge me physically because it was something I felt I really needed help with. Though my test scores showed that I belonged in a more technical occupation specialty, I insisted. They wanted me. When the recruiters from the other branches saw my test scores, they all tried to reel me in but I wanted what I wanted. I wanted to be challenged in a way I had never been challenged before. I got what I asked for, I become a wire systems installer. It meant that I had to learn to gaff poles. I had to run behind 1/2 tons trucks through the swamps to lay cable. I loved it. It felt romantic to me. I also got some things that I had not bargained for. Once I finished training I was most often the only female bodied person in my platoon. This challenged the males and they made no bones about it. At my first duty station the platoon sergeant took it upon himself to teach me that I did not belong where I was. Every weekend that he would assign me to be on duty he would give me the most physically challenging tasks he could think of. He also put me in charge of teaching a class. I believe he was thinking that I would not be up to the task of leading others. Boy was he wrong. Every day most of the other platoon members ridiculed me. They made constant sexist remarks and I dished it back at them. I was tough. But for three months each night, alone in my room, I cried myself to sleep. I was tired, I felt alone and I was still being abused. However, there was no way I was gonna let them see me cry. I was gonna stick it out because I was better than that and I really wanted this. There finally came a day when I had had enough. While I had been in my advanced training courses I was recovering from a broken foot and was temporarily assigned to office duties. I had little to do in the afternoon, but the whole of the UCMJ (military code of justice) sat before me in books. I spent months reading over those books and understanding what my rights and duties were. I knew that what was being done to me was against the code but I didn't want to shake things up. Until I did. I called a meeting between myself, my first sergeant and my platoon sergeant. I was able to quote the violations and was finally able to get my first day off in over three months.

Throughout my time in the army this sort of attitude was the norm towards me but I was also known to be intelligent and not someone to mess with in ways that may get them in trouble. At the same time my superiors saw my potential. I was promoted quickly and I worked hard for it. I wanted my peers to see that I was worthy. Worthy of their admiration. That did not happen in most cases. They often booed and hissed me. They nicknamed me Misery after the film staring Kathie Bates. Most of them feared me but there were those that did admire me. They would skulk to my room when others were not around to see, to ask my advice and sometimes ask for a shoulder to cry on. All the while my heart hurt. But I remained tough. Part of me knew I deserved to be loved but I had no idea how to get the love I so desperately wanted.

During my last year in the army, I was befriended by a married man that I felt really understood me. I was very clear that we were simply friends and I felt that I could be friends with him. He seemed so genuine, open, and stood up for me in public. I thought I had finally found a friend who could really see who I was and who did not care that I was female. That was until one night while having a party in the barracks, I passed out in my room from drinking too much. I awoke to him having pulled my trousers down and trying to get me aroused. I was so angry, I screamed at him to get away from me and get out of my room. He ran out the door and the next Monday I sat him down for a talk. I made it very clear that I was not sexually attracted to him in any way, shape or form. The very thought of having sex with a man that was married with five children made me feel horrible. Shortly after his family came back from Germany and he moved out of the barracks into their new home on post. From then on I was cordial towards him but we were no longer friends. I didn't feel hurt, I simply felt let down and thought it best to stay my distance. A few months later we were walking back to the barracks after morning formation. I had a doctors appointment so I was not participating in physical exercise that day. I didn't ask him why he was not doing so. I simply asked how his wife and children were and talked about the weather. I didn't want to give him any hope that we could become close again. Upon reaching the barracks, he opened the door for me and as I began to walk down the hall, he grabbed me from behind, thrusting his erect penis against my buttocks. I became angry and was very quick to tell him to stop, now. He didn't listen. He grabbed hold of me around my chest from behind, in an effort to keep me from fighting him. But I leaned forward and used my back to flip him onto the floor. It knocked the wind out of him and I used the opportunity to grab and twist his arm. Putting my shoe against his throat, I looked into his eyes and said: "Try it again and you will be very sorry." I thought that was that and I told no one. I had not told anyone about the previous incident either. I had explained it to myself as a miscommunication between us. The 'boys will be boys' message had come across loud and clear during my upbringing and it must be my fault. The second time I knew it had not been my fault but there was a part of me that believed I would be judged and ridiculed. I didn't want that. I wanted to be loved.

A few months later we were both assigned to CQ duty. For those that have never been in the military this is night duty in the office. Basically, someone has to man the phones in case of an emergency and there is cleaning to take care of. I was concerned about this and told the guy I had been dating what was going on. He assured me that he would be by the phone and asked me to call if I needed help. True to form, early in the evening, he made his first move. I was standing at the counter when he grabbed me from behind. I started to fight with him but at that moment another soldier walked into the office. He started to yell at me as if I was doing something wrong. He then joined the other soldier to see about those who had been assigned clean up duty in the back offices. I sat there at a desk contemplating what I should do when he came in and said he was going to check on his kids because his wife was working that night. A minute later all of those that had been assigned clean up duty came to sign out. When I asked them why they were signing out before they finished, they told me he had relieved them of duty. As soon as they left, I made the call to my friend. He must have heard me because before my friend could show up, he came and told me that I could leave.

That night I had a long talk with my friend. For the first time I had someone to talk to about this. Someone that knew me well enough to know I would not lie about such things. I remember his words well. He said to me that while I would be fine because I am tough, he had probably accosted others that were not talking, that I owed it to them, and that to be a good soldier it was my duty to report him. I did and all of my superiors believed me. I initially felt relieved. But that was short-lived. Within two days he had been approached by investigators and the word got out that I was accusing him of assault. I was shunned by almost all my peers. Even the women. Thank goodness that I had a couple of people that were friends, aside from the guy I had been dating who turned out to have a girlfriend in another state that I did not know about.

After a couple of months of investigation, my being belittled at every turn, and feeling afraid most of the time, my battalion commander made an announcement at our monthly meeting. He addressed the entire battalion never using my name but saying that I had more integrity than most of the people he had met. That I was standing up for what it was that we were in the armed forces to fight for. Freedom to be who we are without threat of violence and intimidation. He called for other women to speak up if they were or had been experiencing any sort of assault or sexual harassment. Six of them came forward. All of which said that the man in question had raped them. My best female friend finally spilled the beans too. He had attempted to rape her but someone had walked into the room just in the nick of time. She had been abused for a long time as well but that is her story to tell.

He was convicted of sexual misconduct and given a dishonorable discharge. One would think that I would have felt vindicated by this but I did not. I felt worse. I felt that if I had just spoke up sooner, the others may not have suffered. I felt guilty because I was the strong one, the one able to stand up and fight him off. I had been raised to stand up so why didn't I? It was because I felt that it was all my fault. And then it was my fault that the others had been hurt and everything was my fault. Others assured me it was not but that is not how I felt. Nobody could tell me anything to make it feel like it was not. My conscious mind knew it but my inner child was still very in charge and it was my fault.

So why did I tell you this story in a book about domestic violence? Please bear with me and I will tell you why but there is more to tell before we get to that portion of my experiences and the time when I really began to thrive.

Upon my return home from the army I did not tell my family or friends about what had happened. We didn't discuss these sorts of things in my family, and when asked why I had left after serving my time, I simply said "I realized that it was not a good fit" or that "I wanted to move on to bigger and better things." Just the other day my mother commented that she thought I should have made a career of the army because I was such a good soldier. She asked me again why I left and I simply said that it was not what I wanted for my life. That is very true. All of those statements are true. And I hope you can see why after reading this. What I was looking for upon leaving the army was to heal. I was feeling myself in more and more pain. During the last few months in the military I spent my time going to appointment after appointment because that is what is done when someone gets an honorable discharge. There is a lot of paperwork, different people to see, employment training, doctors appointments, and counseling. Finally, I was getting some counseling but I was afraid to say how I actually felt. It was my fault and I was tough so I would make the most of things. I didn't trust an army counselor. But I digress. I came home and acted like everything was going to be fine. I sought out counseling, jobs and spiritual teaching. I thought that perhaps the reasons that I had kept aligning with these things could be explained by God or some other method. The counselors were a good place to voice how I felt but they rarely offered anything that seemed to really help.

I went to The Spiritualist Church, I went to meditation classes, psychic classes and really, anything I could get my hands on. I also read a lot. I read just about every self help book I could find. Others came to me for advice all the time but when I wanted advice, I was ignored. How could I be so good at helping others but not myself? There had to be something that could make sense of all of this for me. I simply could not continue to keep being the brunt of abuse ,but I could not stop being who I was. I wanted somewhere I could be open and feel free to be who I was. A shoulder to cry on. Others that understood that I was not always tough. Where I could feel safe to be vulnerable. To discover myself more. I had been born with what many call psychic abilities and I largely kept those to myself. I could often see someone that was an obvious cad as they walked into the room. If only I could develop my abilities better, perhaps I could see more. I could learn to protect myself from these things. I knew there had to be a better way and I desperately wanted to find it.

I stayed with my parents the first six weeks after getting home. But my mother wanted to control every step I took. I landed a temporary position right away but the owner of the company turned out to be a tyrant and after two weeks I lost the position. My mother wanted to hear nothing from me about what happened. The only thing she could say to me is that I screwed up again, that I couldn't do anything right. It was late November, and with the holidays right around the corner there was little work available. I wanted to stay home and enjoy my family while etching out a game plan for the 1st of the year. I was receiving more in unemployment than Christmas help would pay, but she insisted that I take a part-time job that paid less than half of what I got in unemployment. After having enough of her incessant need to keep me from enjoying anything in life I finally had enough and got into an argument with her. She kicked me out without a moments notice. I was able to find a friend to stay with for a couple of days and ran into someone that needed a roommate. I didn't have enough money to buy a bed but I thought that at least I had a roof over my head, pillows and blankets. I cleaned the new place top to bottom and spent time writing and making plans for the coming year, and at the beginning of the year I searched for work.

One night, as I sat at a nightclub, I was approached by a woman who I knew from mutual friends. She asked me if I was a dominant, but I had no idea what she meant. Perplexed, I answered that I had been in many leadership roles through my work and in the army. So maybe I did have a dominant personality. She laughed and explained that she was asking me if I liked to tie people up and spank them. I had no idea how she knew this. I had met a couple of males in the army that I had done this with and it was my idea, but I had no idea that people could see this about me. So, she asked if I would like to be paid to attend a party where there would be many men that would like to do my bidding. Nothing sexual was allowed, but spanking and bondage were. I thought to myself, "Wow, I can get paid to do something I enjoy?" I was happy to attend and was paid several hundred dollars to do so. People could not believe that I had never been around others that enjoyed BDSM. I was told over and over again what a natural I was. And it suited me. After a few weeks learning the "ropes" my friend and her boyfriend had a fight, so she invited me in as a business partner. We had parties every weekend and I held private sessions during the week. It took six months or so for me to gain a reputation, but then I started to really clean up. I was the Queen of the Castle and loved every minute of it. Unfortunately, my business partner grew ever more bitter towards me. She was not dominant and worked a full time job. The parties paid all the bills and I manned the phone all day, drew up the ads, and played a great hostess, as well as got all sorts of free labor to finish building things and keep the large house clean. But she wanted to be where I was and she quit her job. Businesses take a bit of time to become somewhat established and it takes a bit of time to establish regular clientele. I explained this but she was convinced that she would be successful right away. When that did not happen she picked fights with me. She began to drink a lot and use methamphetamine. It drove her right over the top and me right out the door.

I got a sales job where I traveled a lot but it did not pay well. After some time my car eventually broke down for the last time and I was stuck hundreds of miles away from friends and family. It was a difficult situation but my grandmother offered to pay for a rental truck so I could tow my car and get myself back to Los Angeles. While staying with my grandmother I landed another sales position, but the territory I was given was getting only one to two appointments a day. This was in pest control for a large company. I went into small businesses and handed them my information, I walked around and left fliers everywhere, but leads did not appear. I had to eventually quit before I ended up owing the company more money than what I was making. I took some temp work when it was available. I looked and looked for work daily. All the while my grandmother criticized me about anything I did. Everything was a toll call but I had to make them or get no work. I paid her but she wanted to control me. I finally figured out where my mother got it from. I purchased prepaid cards and explained it but she insisted that I could not use the phone. I have no idea how I was supposed to get a job without the use of a phone and being very low on money. Until one day, after a very long time spent pounding the pavement, I happened upon a bar that looked like a good place to wind down and have a drink. I was just so stressed and tired of all the hounding. It was there that I met my next short lived relationship. He was charming and had the looks of a young actor. We danced and danced and sang and made love. We had been dating for a couple of weeks when we ran across someone from Phoenix, Arizona that offered us a one bedroom house he wanted to rent out cheap. The only caveat was that we had to fix it up before we could move in. Until that time we could live in his house free of charge. He left first under the pretense of checking things out to make sure all was on the up and up. All the while my grandmother hounded me, and I did continue to look for work just in case. I landed a temporary job but she wanted me home. Finally, I was asked to come to Phoenix, and in my reality it could not have come at a better time. I thought it was fate. In a way I was right. Nothing was going right for me in Los Angeles. When I hit the city limits of Phoenix it was as if a big cloud lifted off of me. A magical feeling hit me. It had nothing to do with my boyfriend at all. It was something else. Something I did not understand at the time.

When I got to the house I was warmly greeted by the owner and my boyfriend but that changed within the week. I had landed a job but I had to wait a week for it to start. Meanwhile, I noticed that things were a bit off. Then when I came home one afternoon, the two of them were nude in the same room together. They had been sleeping together. I had nowhere to go so I decided to simply stay my time until I could get a few paychecks under me and then find a place. But that was not to be. I started sinking because I was in a place where I was once again unwanted. It triggered feelings in me that I had not known I had. I was desperate. I did not eat and barely functioned at all for a week. Nobody seemed to care. They carried on as if I was not there at all. Until one day, I awoke to the feeling of being surrounded.

One of the "gifts" I had always had was that of being able to see spirit. See the dead and all manner of things. What I saw when I woke up did not scare me; I was too depressed for that. It startled me to be sure.

There were five small dark figures surrounding the bed. They did not speak, they did not have to. The energy they gave off was enough. I hid under the covers and I prayed they would leave. They did and I was relieved. Later that day I became suicidal. What I did not understand was that I had already, essentially left my body. I had a prescription from the doctor for steroids and was told that if I took more than one, it could stop my heart. I was planning on taking a handful. I began to write my note to the world when suddenly, I felt myself jolt back into my body. I began to shake and knew that I needed help. So I called the VA psychology hot line and spoke to a counselor. She recommended that I come in first thing in the morning. I did that and put myself in the hospital that day.

I was only in the hospital for three days. The first day was spent not doing much. There was a common area room where I chatted with some of the more coherent patients and made friends with a Hawaiian woman. We could go to the courtyard to get air where others from the hospital were. There we talked and talked. She told me how her mother was a healer and I shared with her my stories of healing animals as a child as well as learning energy healing while part of The Spiritualist Church. It was always pretty instinctive to me. A man overheard our conversation on one occasion and balked. Then he asked me to heal him. I felt where he had been shot. He had a plate in his head and a bullet still lodged in his spine. Because I was able to do that he decided that there must be something to this, so he allowed me to move some energy for him. For the first time since he had been shot in WWII he was able to touch his toes. He thought it was a miracle. And it made me feel better about myself for a minute.

On the second day in the hospital I finally met with a psychiatrist who was quick to diagnose me as bipolar after having talked to me for five minutes. I didn't totally disagree but I asked if we could talk a bit more before he came to any conclusion. He insisted that I should take meds to balance my imbalance in my brain, but I was not convinced. I told him that I was there to face my problems, not to medicate them away. That if he could run a test to show me this imbalance I would be happy to take the meds. He could not and quickly dismissed me. On the fourth morning at the hospital I was called into a meeting. The nursing staff was there as well as two psychologists and the psychiatrist that spoke to me for a total of ten minutes. He spoke and said they had all been observing me for the past three days. They had determined that there was nothing mentally wrong with me. That I simply had to learn that I could not save the world.

I again had nowhere to go. So I went down to the courtyard to talk with fellow vets. One of whom I had made friends with. I told him what happened and he offered me a place on his sofa. I stayed on that sofa for a week with no energy to do much. I did try to get out and over to the VA where I could at least talk with someone, because my gracious host suffered from severe PTSD and the new medications he was on caused him to sleep most of the time. About two weeks into this great depression I went to see a doctor to get a check up. I waited and waited for my appointment for 3 hours before a nurse came out and told me that I would not be seen that day. When I tried to reschedule I was told that I would have to come back to do that. No reasons given. I snapped. I began to cry. I was again feeling completely unwanted and I was desperate for help, but it seemed that nobody was there to help me. I had seen one counselor since my stay at the hospital, but I felt like this person was just there to placate me. It felt as if there was no help at all for me.

I made my way to the courtyard again and it was strangely empty. Only one lone guy was there smoking a cigarette in the middle of the afternoon. I sat down on a bench and began to cry. I became angry and filed with dismay. I started yelling, "why? why?" I only ever wanted to be loved and to be of help to the world. I have tried every thing I know to try to get help but there is none. I give up, I completely give up. You show me what I need to do God, because, I am obviously clueless. It's hard to convey but I felt a release of energy in that moment that was incredible. Then I felt an energy come up to meet it. For the first time in a long time, I knew I was going to be OK. What I didn't know at the time was that this was my first step to awakening and becoming more conscious of actual love. It was my first step towards self-love.

A few minutes after I had this experience I sat down with someone that I had spoken with on several occasions. He looked at me and asked when the last time was I had something to eat. It had been a couple of days. He was there for group therapy and asked me to meet him at a restaurant up the street in an hour to have lunch. I obliged. At lunch he started to talk to me about things that rang true. The basics of why I was feeling like I was. He told me I should meet with his roommates because he thought that I would learn a lot from them. Learn a lot? That was an understatement. We arrived at 3pm in the afternoon and I was introduced to the man that I felt I could talk to. I didn't know why I felt so comfortable with him but I knew that I did. I felt as if I could say anything to him. I was not judged. Instead; I was met with understanding. I told him of many of my "psychic" experiences. I only half believed some of them. They made sense to my heart but my brain often thought I must be insane. But he listened and he believed me. Then his wife came home. She at first seemed a bit stand offish to me, but not uncaring. She had a long day but still joined in for a bit. She started to tell me of other ways I could help myself and that she may be able to help me. That there were many things I needed to work on, that many did not understand love and wanting to actually be happy and whole. What I had been doing all along was listening to my heart. I had simply not been given the tools to be able to follow it properly. I stayed there till the wee hours of the morning chatting and learning. I could not get enough. It was magical and I knew with every fiber of my being that I had found what I was looking for.

When I arrived back at the place where I was staying I was accused of being out with a man, of going out partying. I tried to explain where I was and that I didn't want to call late to wake him up but it fell on deaf ears. I had never said or done anything to make this man feel like he was involved with me in any way and yet he was behaving as if we were in some sort of relationship. He threatened me and said some of the most awful things to me that anyone could say to someone. He asked me to leave but I had nowhere to go. So I called Mary and explained what was going on. Maybe there was some way to deal with him; I had no idea. I was so lost and confused, depressed and out of my mind. She offered for me to come stay with her. Later she told me that she knew that if she did not, I would have probably died. I know she was right.

I spent the next couple of months recovering. I read many self-help books, joined Co-Dependents Anonymous and showed up at meetings every other day. And I meditated. I meditated, I ate foods that were healthy, organic and alive. For the first time ever I found people that really supported me. All they asked was that I worked on myself. That I work as hard as I could to heal. They guided me, giving me support, showing me the talents that I already had. Above all else, I was loved unconditionally. They were both quite impressed with how I was able to come so far so quickly. It was often painful, I would vomit, sweat, sometimes see stars. I had to purge, and purge I did. Always with the love and support of those around me. I got a job and began to really function. There was lots of pain but I knew that at each painful step, each time I was able to truly express who I was, I was a little bit freer.

I finally decided to join a local ashram. I knew I wanted to be surrounded by unconditional love and help others. There I became the head gardener. I studied herbals and more energy healing, and I healed more every day. I walked in a state of meditation and I loved. Boy did I love. I was so happy and I had never felt more free. I helped many in the community with all manner of challenges and they helped me. We shared any and everything. There was no space for judgment of others. There were challenges but they were met with love. We were sometimes sad, angry and hurt. We did not ignore these feelings because they are and were a part of who we are. We met them from a space of compassion. I did not feel like anything could not somehow be accomplished. I had many so many visions and insights. Everything just flowed so well. It was the most magical two years of my life. Looking back on it, I think it was the childhood that I missed out on the first time around.

At the end of two years I began to feel like I was being limited in some way. In my meditations I was being shown that it was time to move forward. But what did moving forward mean? I was happy and content. I was always working on myself and moving forward. Then I began to realize that if I was going to move forward I had to leave my new-found family. That meant going out into the world. My teachers and

I agreed. I had outgrown the space to be where I was. I felt that their teachings were wonderful but something inside me longed for more. Longed for a way to grow further. I had no idea what that meant but I knew I had a lot of faith in the universe. I trusted the universe to take care of me. So with only $800 in my pocket, I left. In Phoenix there were rooms for rent on a weekly bases that were comfortable and clean. I took one of those and began looking for a job and a truck rental to move my things. While pricing truck rentals I heard a voice say to me, "Ask how much it would cost to go to San Diego." I did, and low and behold, it was much less expensive to rent a truck for three days and go to San Diego. It was the universe speaking to me loud and clear.

I picked up my belongings and headed out of town. I felt more free than I ever had. I knew I was headed in the right direction for myself because I had faith. Upon arriving in San Diego I stopped off to get some food that I had to wait to be prepared. When I stepped outside I saw a man on a pay phone. He stood out to me so I waived hello. We struck up a conversation and I told him that I was on my way to the ashram gardens in Encinitas to figure out what my next move was. He had been on the phone to his girlfriend. She was coming to pick him up after work. They were staying in a halfway house and he invited me to come stay, free of charge, for two weeks. I was grateful and happy. I had faith and was being taken care of. I found a job within the next week and within two weeks had two jobs. I managed to rent a room in a residential hotel. It was a bit sleazy but I didn't care.

I had love and faith. This lasted a month before I was accused of having men in my room. I had one visitor the whole time for an hour; he was a friend. I got on the phone to a co-worker who had a neighbor that was in need of a roommate so, I moved in. My plan was to save money for a car and then move into my own place. But after a several months my new roommate made moves on me. When I declined he threw me out. I didn't know where I was to go. I had managed to buy a car and was still working two jobs. I decided to go to the park and meditate on what I should do. Staying in my car was an option but renting a room was not. I didn't want a repeat of what had happened at the last place. I almost had enough money to get my own apartment and I didn't want to dip into that money either. That day I met a lovely woman that was giving psychic readings in the park. I walked over to her thinking that I perhaps she could help me with a reading. But she looked up at me and tears began to well in her eyes. She said she saw the beauty of my presence. It was something she had rarely seen. And she began to say "Yogananda, Yogananda. He loves you so much." When she calmed down she explained to me that she was seeing Paramahansa Yogananda standing next to me. She then knew she had to help me. When I told her what had happened she took me to meet her roommate. They decided to allow me to sleep on their sofa for a few weeks. I did, and within two weeks I found an apartment that I could afford in a nice area of town. I never gave up. I did what I had to do and I had faith that things would work out. They did. They did so in what some may find to be miraculous ways. During those weeks I also found one full-time job that paid enough to sustain me. It was customer service/sales at a popular fitness company.

I worked that job for a year until one day I heard the universe whisper to me. I want you to use your gifts. So I began to do readings professionally at a local spiritual shop, and at times, in the park while working at my job. This did not go very well. I noticed that many of those performing the same thing as I was were playing into the pains that people often came to me with. I felt that simply reading what was going on and what the energies were saying was the most likely outcome was fleeting at best. I had lots of tools. I had been trained in spiritual arts, studied world religions on many levels but there was something missing. I quit doing this and took a massage therapy course. Having done this I pulled away from my comfortable job. I loved my job but this energy overtook me. There was still doubt stirring in me and I became depressed for a few days. I meditated and meditated and I cried. There was a big part of me that wanted to be like everyone else. But it was clear that this was not my path. To work every day at a job was not my path. I quit my job and went into healing and massage full-time, however, I was coming up short on my bills. I mediated and meditated about this for months, until I realized that there was a lot more money to be made as an adult service provider.

I balked at the idea at first. It was morally wrong. But something said to me that there were ways to do things that could be done in a way that was healing for me and my clients. I gathered all my courage and welcomed my first client. It was actually freeing and loving. A wonderful experience, and I was paid well. I had always been a sexual person and my energy was such that I could really help those that were in need of love. I know this may sound mad to many. This is the first time I am publicly writing about this. But it was true. At this phase of my journey, it was freeing and loving. I was particular about those that I would see. When I got calls I explained that I approached things from a space of love. And I did. I became very successful because many men were looking for something more than just a physical release. They were searching for someone they could trust with their secrets, their desires. They wanted to feel loved for who they actually were as opposed to what they showed the world. And I gave them that. I gave them a safe space to be loved unconditionally, to explore themselves in a safe space. There is much more to being a good adult service provider than one may think. It's not always a seedy business. I am not alone in this. I have met with and befriended many others that approach things in similar ways. The men I saw gave a lot to me for the services that I provided, and I was never embarrassed of what I did. I certainly did not go around advertising it to those at school and in social circles. People got to know me pretty well before I told them what I did. And those that got to know me could not judge what I did. I wasn't a drug addict or someone that was always looking to get attention. I was strong and empowered to a great extent.

This also freed me to go back to school and pursue my studies. I looked around at what it was I wanted to study. Taking into account my talents and what may serve to make a good living. I decided on interior architecture. I could work for myself and use my creative abilities. I applied to a school that is considered one of the best in the world. People come from all over to study design here, but they only teach design and allow a total of 300 students at a time. I was amazed that within a week after applying I was accepted. I loved design and excelled greatly. I was a favored student. And when I was diagnosed with cancer, a friend spread the news around campus. I was approached by many that had never had a conversation with me in the past. They all expressed the feeling of inspiration that my presence in classes gave them. I had no idea that I was doing this for others. I was simply following my heart.

Before I talk to you about my stint with cancer, I want to discuss a relationship that I had in the interim. About 2 years after leaving the ashram and well into my courses, I started acupuncture treatments for my thyroid and to regulate my menstrual cycle. I had gone to the doctor for a check up on my thyroid (I had been diagnosed with hypothyroid disease at the age of 25). She was amazed that my thyroid seemed to be miraculously getting a lot better and cut my medication in half. She advised me that she was leaving the clinic but to make sure I had another appointment within the month because cutting the medication down like this was a bit risky. A few weeks later I met a guy. I remember the meeting well. I had been to a local festival and was walking home when I noticed this guy sitting at a table in front of a restaurant. His aura beamed with light. I had never seen such light emanating from someone before. I waived hello and he invited me to come over. So I sat down for a chat. We made a date for the next day. The connection during that date was one I had never felt before. It was magical. I thought I had died and gone to heaven. The sex was amazing, loving and unbridled. He moved in with me within weeks. I was trusting the universe, and while I definitely had some challenges, I felt as if I was able to overcome anything. Little by little as I got to know him I realized that something was amiss. He wanted sex less, he lied a lot, and pulled away from me often. We began to argue. I pleaded with him to simply learn to love himself. I had lost the balance I had worked so hard to continue with. I felt like I was going a bit insane, so I made an appointment to see a therapist. She diagnosed me as being bipolar. I questioned that because I had worked so hard on not looking for any major highs or lows. I also brought up the fact that my appointments to check my thyroid count kept getting rescheduled by the clinic, even though I pleaded with staff to explain the importance of the problem. I went to group counseling, individual therapy and took the medications that were prescribed, but things grew worse and the medication seemed to make me feel worse. After two months on the medication, I stopped taking it and I broke it off with my boyfriend. There were just too many lies and I could not be with someone I felt I could not trust.

I agreed to allow him to stay with me rent-free for six weeks as he had nowhere to go. He was working but he needed time to save money. I thought I was simply being the loving and caring person that I knew I was. I simply asked that he respect my place and my space, pick up after himself, and try to get some help. A week later I found out he had quit his job and had a woman in my house while I was at school. I talked to him but he seemed to have no qualms about what he was doing. He seemed to think that I should simply allow him to stay. It was over between us and I wanted to move on. A few nights later he stayed gone all night. I paged him to find out whether he was coming back or not but got no reply. The next morning I paged him several times but again, I got no reply. Anger welled up in me. I felt used and hurt. I packed his things into duffel bags and waited for him to return. He did the next afternoon. I explained why I was kicking him out in a very calm tone but he was irate. I asked that we sit down and have a conversation because in my mind I simply wanted closure and to move forward. He accused me of being nuts and there was certainly some truth to that. It had been difficult for me to not be extremely emotional at times during the past few months. I told him that I did not want for him to come back again, I was done and I didn't want anything to be left in the energy between us. He snapped when he heard this and attacked me. I fought back but he was eventually able to pin me down on the bed. I will never forget the look in his eyes as he was choking me. I hit him in the face over and over again but it did nothing. He was on top of me, choking me. Finally he said, "I am going to kill you." His voice sounded like pure evil to me. At that moment I was overcome with a feeling of love. My heart burst open. I don't know how I was able to speak but I gasped, "Go ahead, kill me, I am not afraid." I wasn't afraid at all. I was empowered in that moment. He let go. I yelled for him to get out but he insisted on going through his things. I yelled again and threatened to call the police. He threw the phone at me but I didn't want to call the police. I just wanted him gone. I became angry and threw the bags I had packed over the balcony of my apartment. I shouted for him to just go. I hung the phone back up and looked at it contemplating whether to call the police. But before I got the chance he had dialed 911.

I listened as he told the operator that I had attacked him. That he needed help. I shouted that he had attacked me. When the police showed up he was outside. They spoke to him and to me about what had happened. I told them how he had attacked me and that I simply wanted him to leave. I didn't want to press any charges, I just wanted to be done with the whole thing. I wanted to heal and move forward. I was not the type to hold grudges and didn't think that punishing someone was the answer. They asked me over and over where the phones in the apartment were. I pointed them out but was confused why they kept asking me this. They asked me what would happen if they simply left and I said that I hoped nothing. All he had to do was leave. I didn't want any trouble. I will never forget my astonishment as they put handcuffs on me. I was 32 years old and I had never been in any sort of legal trouble. I was not a violent person. I had spent years working on self-love and expressing unconditional love towards others. Why was this happening to me? I felt utterly powerless and betrayed in ways by the universe. I was a helper and a healer. Why? Why had I been betrayed. I only wanted to experience the oneness with all.

Once in the back of the police car the officers explained to me that they did not believe him but they had to do their job. He was claiming that I had attacked him and wanted to press charges. They took me to the station in an effort to talk to their commanding officer, to try to convince him that I didn't belong in jail. Unfortunately, he did not listen, so I was carted off to county jail. I wept the entire ride. The pain I was experiencing was overwhelming. I could not help but cry. No matter what I did, it would not stop. I found out what my charges were while being processed into jail. Assault and battery as well as false imprisonment. I was put into a dormitory with around 60 felons. I had never been in such a situation and didn't know what to do, but I wept. I just kept on crying with very little time to breathe. I tried to meditate but every time I closed my eyes I saw pain, I saw war, I saw famine, I saw murder, rape and all manner of what can be considered to be the devastation that humans do. This lasted for three days. I did not sleep. On the first day I had a visitor. I was handed a restraining order and accused of all the things that were done to me. I could not believe this. Thank goodness for my friends in the spiritual community that had known me for quite some time. They assured me that I would be OK and helped me to keep my strength. This was a challenge but one I could overcome. They knew I was telling the truth. Apparently so did the police officers that had arrested me. When I finally had my day in court, I did not have to stand in front of a judge. All charges had been dropped. It was obvious to them that these were all lies. My best friend came to pick me up that night. Thank goodness she was so loving. She was the woman that had allowed me to stay on her sofa when I first got into town. She knew me to be strong and loving. Thank goodness as well that when I got to my home, he was gone. It was obvious that he had stayed there while I was in jail. There were dirty towels and most of the food was gone. A day later, I finally had my appointment to rectify the problem with my thyroid medication. It only took a week for me to feel more balanced. I was not bipolar.

A few days after that I had an appointment with my gynecologist to have a laser procedure in order to remove the cancer cells that he had found in my pap smear. The doctor announced as he finished the procedure that I was all cured. But something inside me said that there was something amiss. I felt like there was something in my body that had been missed. When my friend called to see how it had gone I said to her that I felt like I had tumors. I didn't know why but I felt it.

I meditated on this and then decided, that if they were actually there I would deal with it, that it may simply be my mind playing tricks on me. I waited for the letter in the mail for my test results but a few days later I got a phone call instead. I was asked to come in the next day for a follow up appointment. That the doctor wanted to make sure that everything was healing. I obliged and was directly escorted into the doctor's office instead of the examining room. I felt nervous but breathed into a calm state. Then he told me. The pathologist had found a different kind of cancer cell near the top of where he had cut a piece of my cervix off. This sort of cell was very aggressive and I would need to have a hysterectomy. I was put through a series of tests that showed that I had tumors in my uterus. It spent two months going through tests and waiting for my operation. I mourned my life as I was told by the oncologist that my chances of beating this were about 20%. That the type of cells presented were normally associated with ovarian cancer. I researched and I meditated. I saw my acupuncturist and took herbs. I meditated for hours on end to melt those tumors and the cancer away. I felt helpless at first, then I became angry, and finally I was ready to fight from a space of love.

I remember sitting on my front porch and thinking about all the people that had said they were praying for me. This was prior to social media and yet, I had people from every faith I could think of praying for me. I realized I had touched the lives of many, many people. I realized that I had lived a very full life. I had traveled pretty extensively, I had studied and participated with all manner of people - from the famous to the down trodden. I had studied and participated in so many forms of healing that I lost count. If it was my time to leave I was OK with that, I lost all fear of death. However, if I was meant to stay, I certainly had the energy and backing to do so. I walked back into the living room and sat on the sofa feeling relieved and like I had just purged something huge. Then I felt a gentle hand touch my shoulder and I heard a whisper. The voice said, "There is still too much work to be done." I began to cry and knew that I was meant to stay. I would survive this and I was choosing to do so with love.

Two weeks later I had my surgery. Upon being returned to my room, my surgeon came in to tell me how it went. Right away I asked him if they got all the tumors. He was astounded that I knew. You see, he never told me about them. He didn't want me to be too frightened. He looked at me and said, "There were no tumors." Then he asked me what happened to them. I smiled and said I had meditated them away. He smiled and told me he believed me. Then he explained that he was astounded to find that I only had a microscopic amount of cancer left when the surgery was performed. That the chances of it ever coming back were so slim that I should never give it a thought. I spent a week on the cancer ward of that hospital because my body kept rejecting the pain medication. But I smiled the whole time. I had beat it and I was free. There was still much work left to be done. The nurses visited me and remarked at how I was probably the most positive patient they had ever seen on that ward. Pretty soon they began to ask my advice about things in their own lives. About how I managed to remain so positive and loving through this. I helped them and they made sure I was well taken care of. The day I left the hospital it was the first day of spring. All the flowers had come into bloom. As I rode through town in my parents car I saw how magical the world was. It sparkled with new possibility for me. When I tell people that I had cancer, they often try to console me but I don't feel any need for that. It was one of the most important lessons of my life. It freed me from a worry about death and renewed me in ways that I cannot express enough. And the whole abusive situation that lead up to it was quite useful in giving me the strength to survive. I realized that I had aligned with what I had aligned with to give me strength. I had been wanting to truly feel the oneness for a long time and I had on many levels, but when I was shown the darkest parts of humanity I was even more in touch with the oneness of this planet. I had no time to mourn my short lived relationship, but there was no need. He was a catalyst to my expanded awareness and my healing. As I healed my cancer, I healed the anger and the pain of my incarceration and the betrayal. I had to, in order to move forward and survive.

A few months after surgery I decided to move back to Los Angeles. I was hearing a calling, and while I was not yet finished with my studies at the school I had been attending, I could not wait any longer. I enrolled at a similar school in Los Angeles but it was not a good fit. I felt like a failure. What had happened? I loved architecture. I spent the summer exploring why. I dated and had wonderful experiences as well as some that we a bit challenging but nothing earth shattering. I explored my sexuality as well. I was always exploring myself and others through sexuality, through the study of spirituality, religion, psychology; I wanted to know why people did what they did. It had always been my biggest question in life. People often confused me and the pain that was felt was something I often questioned. I felt deep pain but I felt deep joy. I did my best to practice non-attachment and I was very good at it. I always thought positively. I thought that all I had to do was to override my subconscious with my consciousness. I could master this. I just knew I could. I had a few short lived relationships that were healthy but just not the fit that I was looking for. They ended amicably. I am still in touch with several of them. We will always be friends. We shared some deep experiences in sharing and practicing polyamory. I loved the idea of being free to love.

I explored what I could do with a degree in art history and ran across information on utilizing it to become an archaeologist. Archaeology sang to my heart. It appealed to my nerd and almost everything I had studied thus far. I asked myself how I had never considered it before. So I took myself to Pasadena City College and began to study art history. I took studio classes in art, math, science and history courses. I loved every minute of it and was often taught by successful artists and scientists from Jet Propulsion Laboratory. I took a couple of beginning courses in anthropology because I began to understand that archaeology was best studied within the context of anthropology. By the time I transferred to Cal State Northridge I was primed. I had an excellent background. One of my first professors had two PhD's in art history and anthropology. He was an archaeologist teaching art history. He convinced me that I needed to double major and he was correct. It only took me adding one semester to earn two degrees and it gave me a competitive edge for graduate school.

I poured myself into my studies. I could not get enough. I studied biology, history, art, geology, psychology, economics and more. Here I was, studying everything that I had ever dreamed of with some of the foremost experts in their fields. They challenged me and I met each challenge with vigor and zest. I was in love. In love with the study of human behavior. Meanwhile, I met a man from India that was fourteen years younger than I. We became quick friends, hanging out all the time. He had just graduated with an MA in Nanotechnology. We had a lot to talk about and very much enjoyed ourselves. I didn't dream of getting too involved with him because he was so much younger and from a different culture, but my friends and family insisted that he would be good for me. They were right. He was wonderful. I trusted him implicitly. We had a very unconditional, loving relationship for two years. We almost married. We had been discussing it but I knew that he wanted children and I could not have them. That and I was already over 40. I played with the concept of adoption but it was not meant to be. It was far too expensive an option. One night I sat him down and asked him if he wanted children or if he felt that he needed them because of societal pressure. I did not expect an immediate answer. The next day he came to visit and told me that he actually wanted them. We cried a bit but both knew it was best to end the romantic part of our relationship. We also agreed that we would always love and support each other. To this day we do. He has been one of my rocks since I met him and my family have adopted him as their own. He was married last year. It was one of the most joyous marriages I have ever experienced. I have only ever wanted him to be happy and he is.

But I digress. As part of my studies I was required to attend field school. I was very happy to be accepted to a special field school in Turkey. I had put an emphasis in Anatolian archaeology during my undergrad studies. Not only was I accepted to a field school program with only eight students but I received a grant from my school to pay for it. We traveled to fourteen different archaeology sites that summer and spent time working with archaeologists at all 14 of them. It was the opportunity of a lifetime. Nobody had ever heard of such an elaborate field school but all the archaeologists that we talked with wished they had been fortunate enough to have had an opportunity like it. Many of those we met with were impressed with my abilities. Particularly as someone that had just finished their undergrad. They sometimes pulled me aside and asked what my plans were for the future. I had already been accepted to a program at the school I had been attending so I continued on there. While in school my professors kept advising me to to teach. But I had an aversion to teaching college. It didn't quite feel like the right fit but I did eventually come around to the idea of it.

During my last year in school I had been asked to come to Middle Eastern Technical College in Ankara, Turkey. It is the MIT of the middle east. I would be within 2 hours drive of some of the most prolific archaeology sites in the world. I gladly accepted but that spring I became sick. The doctors seemed to think that it was my gallbladder yet, I had symptoms that were not explained and there were no blockages. I was scheduled to return to Turkey for the summer and was given the go ahead from the GI specialist. They had put me through test after test but could not figure out what the matter was. As long as I ate a low fat diet, I should be OK. Removing my gallbladder could wait a couple of months. I was pursuing my dreams and the docs didn't seem to think it was that crucial. The night I returned home I began to vomit green bile so I went to the emergency room. It was determined that my gallbladder had become severely infected. I spent a week in the hospital with no food and rounds of antibiotics that were given intravenously. My gallbladder was finally removed three weeks later and I was out of pain. But that only lasted a couple of weeks.

I woke up one morning to an excruciating pain in my back. It would shoot up and fill the whole of the right side of my body. I was weak. I could barely get out of bed. Even getting up to eat or do dishes made me feel as if I had run a marathon on most days. The migraines I had since I was a child became more frequent (at least once a week) and more intense. They had done this over a long amount of time. I was largely bed ridden. Blood tests revealed that I was very low in vitamin D and B-12. So I took supplements. I researched when I could see well enough to do so. I felt like I was dying. I could literally feel my organs shutting down. I ate little and worked when I had a bit of energy. I was a mess and I knew that if I did not do something, I would die a slow painful death. One day while at the health food store a woman gave me an article on gluten poisoning that was written by a physician. I had GI tests and blood tests to see if this was the cause but they came back negative. I went to see my doctor but he stopped testing me for anything. The look on his face was one of despair. He just shrugged and said he could think of nothing else to test me for. After months of this suffering I ran across an article that said that the tests for celiac disease can often give a false negative. So out of desperation I quit eating gluten. In a few days by pain got a lot better. My energy began to return and I was on the road to recovery. I went to the doctor and told him about it. He did some research and discovered that sometimes false negatives do happen. I changed my diet in many ways and within a month I was starting to feel like myself again. I had kept in touch with my supervisor for schooling but I had missed getting into the program on time and I was now out of money.

Between the economy and having been sick, I had lost most of my clients but I held on. My car was repossessed when I had only three payments left. I looked for work and tried to contact the professors but was largely ignored. They gave up on me. I sunk into depression but I worked when I could. I had friends that helped as well. Thank goodness for them. I don't think I would have made it without their help. I was crushed but had little time to do much about it. I tried to meditate and heal. I had put ten years of my life into becoming an archaeologist but it was all for nothing. I was so close. I had earned things that many only dream of and I failed. To make matters worse, when I went to eat out, I was often met with a sort of disdain because I could not eat gluten. It really hurt. It hurt because I almost died and almost lost everything due to gluten poisoning. I was already feeling horrible so it was hard to not become angry. I worked to see the positive in this but I just couldn't see it. I looked for ways to better myself. I took up being a dominant again. It appealed to me once more. Not that I had ever been sexually submissive. I was raised to believe that I was supposed to enjoy sex and if I wasn't, there was something wrong, but not with me.

I started to gain more clients and was able to barely pay my bills. I kept hoping and praying that I would find what my next move would be but I felt utterly betrayed by the universe. Why would I be lead down a road that would only lead me to failure and not from my own doing? I was a loving person and I thought I was more empowered than this. The answers to that did not come for a few years.

I began seeking out a romantic partner that I could be casual with. I wanted someone to connect with but I knew I was in no shape for a full relationship. However, something inside me wanted to feel this intense connection that I could sense was right was around the corner. I was in a big transitional state. I could feel that as well. I started to feel my heart opening more and more after a time. I worked hard for it. I met quite a few people but none were a good fit. There was one that I was a bit stricken with but she had many issues. I really just wanted to help. After a few months of seeking, I had given up for the moment, when a friend called and invited me to a party. I declined at first but she insisted that I needed to get out because I had not done so in a couple of weeks. I agreed and went to the party.

While sitting outside I felt an energy. My friend sat next to me. I asked her if she felt it as well but she did not. I had no idea what it was but it felt pleasant. Then I looked over and there she stood on the steps. I looked over at my friend and said, "There it is. That is what I have been looking for." She went inside and within minutes came over to introduce herself. She was sweet and sensitive. I played a bit coy but we exchanged social media. Throughout the night we chatted a bit here and there. I spent the next couple of weeks stalking her online and later found out that she did me as well.

When we next met the energy was unmistakably intense. I was more drawn to her than I had ever been to anyone in my life. This both excited and concerned me. But something was telling me that I was supposed to be with her. So I made a move and asked her to come chat with me in private. We did and when we first kissed, it felt like the magic explained in great works of poetry and novels. We spent every weekend together for the next three months. On the third weekend we had a chat about the energy felt and both agreed that we didn't know what it was, it was more intense than either of us had ever experienced and we were both in our 40's. We also agreed that for our own reasons, neither of us wanted to be in a committed relationship. But the energy had something else in mind. We were simply drawn to each other.

My business started to fail more and more. I could not get enough clients to pay my bills. And I could find no work that paid enough to make things work either. Eventually, I lost my apartment, so I opted to stay at a shelter for homeless veterans. While there I landed a job working for a political advocacy group but it was not enough to make a living. I loved what I was doing and looked for more work. I had occasional professional domination sessions but I was still not earning enough to even pay for a roommate situation. While at the shelter, my food was often stolen. There was a lot of fighting. I was working until 9:30pm, did not get to bed until 10:30 or 11 and normally fell to sleep around 12, but I had to be up at 5am and have chores done by 6am. We were not allowed inside between 8am and 5pm. I was instructed to go to appointments that were designed for people with drinking or drug problems and people with no job at all. I spent most of my time during the day, hanging out in the courtyard between appointments before I had to go to work at 1pm. I missed my freedom but I told myself I could stick it out. When I had time I would go over to my girlfriend's house and search for jobs on her computer. There were few at the shelter on dial-up and I had to wait around for hours to use those on most days. One night, I just could not take it anymore. I had been with her for an hour that night because I had no work. I called to talk to her about how I was feeling about being left out, feeling worthless and jealous but she never answered. I was a mess. I could not sleep, I felt so alone in that room and I could not get up to watch television or go for a walk. I felt like I could not breathe. I left. I got into my car and left. I was used to driving around when I felt like this but if I returned I would have been kicked out anyway. I made my way to my girlfriend's house. It was 3am. I was crying and tried to explain how I felt but she was angry. Understandably so.

For the next fifteen months I worked on getting a place of my own. The system made it very difficult. I also went to many job interviews and put in resumes wherever I could. I had no luck. I became sick often. I would recover for a month or so and become sick with a cold again and again. To the point where my boss took me aside to ask if I had a health problem I was hiding. I was very stressed and confused. Each time it seemed that I could catch a break, find a place to live, find a better job or a second job, something would happen. Things that seemed beyond my control. I remember having a conversation with a friend who said that it was like I kept sliding on a banana peel. That was a very good analogy.

I thought that all I had to do was be tough the way I had been in the past. The ashram had shown me how to be softer, more loving and I worked with that. But the other aspects of myself came forward. Things I had no idea even existed. I did not recognize myself. I said mean things towards my girlfriend on many occasions and she did towards me. I remember telling her on several occasions that this was not me. I never acted like this in my life. That strong connection also meant that I could feel everything she felt almost as if it were my own. Things grew ever more toxic. I just wanted to be loved but I had lost all my love for myself. I fought and fought but I became more abusive towards her and she towards me. She broke up with me during a very heated argument. I had never felt so crushed. It felt like someone was ripping me apart from the inside.

I stayed there for another month before I was finally able to find a place. It was pretty miraculous how that happened. I did want to move all along. I never wanted to be somewhere that I was not wanted. And she did not want to live with me. I do not blame her for that at all.

I tried to be friends with my now ex. She had decided to take in a roommate with someone that had stalked me. She knew this and told me she wanted us all to be friends. I understand that she is a very forgiving and loving person but to be friends with someone that came after me because I did not want to be romantically involved with them was too much for me. I was hurting and needed space. We went to a movie together where I told her that I wanted to cut ties for a few months. She asked me why I hated the roommate so much. My answer was that she was not the one I felt hate for. She was not the one who betrayed me. I simply wanted the roommate out of my life. As was her way, she refused to acknowledge what I was saying and began to walk away. What I had not realized was that I had held a lot back. I stopped her by standing in front of her car door and I ripped into her for thirty minutes. I was crying and telling her what I felt were her problems. About the way I felt she treated me and the fact that she had never apologized for anything she had done towards me. I felt utterly powerless and angrier than I had ever felt in my life. But she wasn't listening. She called the police and we both left. I was nuts and wanted some of the things I had left at her house. I felt like I was done. I just wanted to be done with all of this and move on. I followed her in my car. It was insane. What I really wanted was some semblance of control. My life was so out of control. I had no idea what to do. So I tried to control the person that I had loved the most.

I could tell you all the things that she did and did not do. They would be true but that is her story to tell. The thing is that this relationship was the most pivotal point of my life. Why? Because unknown to me consciously, I had a lot of issues to handle. I had handled them in the past in various ways but they were more surface than I had imagined. In this relationship I came to feel what it feels like to truly be the one that is looking to control another through whatever means necessary. I became the one that people call the abuser. There was certainly plenty of abuse to be had on both sides but I could and only can clean my own plate.

I spent the next year looking for help. I went to a couple of counselors but they only wanted to look at the mental surface of things. I had already done that. I had spent years writing in journals and mentally understanding my childhood. I had spent a lot of time in meditation and clearing energies. I tried to handle this in the same ways but it didn't work. I had many vivid nightmares. Every time I tried to avoid her in public she would show up. If she didn't physically show up, there were reminders everywhere. A big part of me wanted to let go but my heart could not. To let go of her meant to let go of my heart.

Finally, in my seeking, I found a spiritual teacher that talked about finding core traumas and beliefs. I soaked up her writing and videos like a sponge. The main thing she taught was to go deep into feelings. Through the heart. That we could access the original feelings there. There was no need to think about where they came from or question what they were. We could then go in and empower our child. The actual child that lived deep within our being. I had done regression therapy in the past and had even gone deep to try to heal my inner child. But this was a bit different. With only a couple of tweaks, I was able to really empower my inner child. To the point where I completely grew up. But this was only the beginning of my healing. With all of those false programs of being unworthy, less than, abandoned, not good enough, unloved, I began to truly see.

I saw that there were no victims or perpetrators. That there was nobody to blame. That I was not to blame, my mother was not to blame. Everybody was playing with the tools that they had access to. I saw that I could truly choose to be happy and free. That the only love I ever needed was my own. I simply had limited access to it in the past. I could be vulnerable because if I did get triggered, I had new ways to deal with that and my triggers were mine. That I aligned with everything in my life in order to heal myself. All of this time I had spent protecting myself was actually causing me to seek out harm. And much of the harm I experienced was because I did not trust myself. After all, how could I love myself if I did not trust myself?

I have not been sick a day in the past two years. I still have moments when sickness knocks at my door but I am able to heal it quickly. I am open and trusting. I don't ignore things at all. The world still has a lot of pain to grow through as do I. But I welcome the pain to heal myself. I don't push it away. I know it's there to show me what I need to be shown for my expansion and for the expansion of others that choose to align with me.

I have figured out what all of this was about and what each phase of my life was for. How it served me and how I can continue to use each part as a service to myself and to the world. I am never ashamed of anything because I don't judge myself which in turn, helps me to not judge others. I certainly observe. I do my best not to ignore a thing but I have learned non-resistance on a level that I could not imagine in the past. I integrate all parts of my life and live in the moment. I love myself unconditionally. That in turn allows me to truly love others. And I am surrounded by those that know how to love unconditionally. Or is it that I can allow others to love me unconditionally? I think both are true. But the best part is that I get to show others how to love themselves unconditionally.

I can feel the unconditional love that my parents have for me and I understand them as well as others on very deep levels. There is nobody to blame so there is no need to forgive and no need to judge. This has allowed me to truly open up and be there as a life coach and a healer in ways I never dreamed possible.

The reason I spent so many years studying human behavior in all of it's forms is so I could incorporate this into my work. So I could truly understand duality and process my way through it. So I could look at the world as the grand collective that it is and revel in it's beauty. I understand why I was born to my parents. My mother is strong and resilient. She taught me things that nobody else could. I grew up with men that were strong enough to be vulnerable and truly love. My dad is one of them. Like cancer these relationships help me to form who I am today. I have chosen to learn and grow from them. I have chosen to look at things from all sides. And when I awake on a morning where I may feel a bit cranky, my first response is "Not today Satan, not today." Today I choose to be happy and live in a space of love. To meet each challenges the best I can. It's all up to me.

We certainly all need help and I have had and do have mine. I wrote this chapter in an effort for others to know that they are not alone. Each of us has a similar journey. No person is without pain. For instance; I may not have stayed in one relationship where I was being physically harmed. Instead, I chose multiple relationships and played things out on a different level each time. I didn't understand that choosing to leave each time I had enough but choosing a toxic situation over and over again is not much different than staying in one toxic relationship for a long amount of time. I didn't know my way out of this loop but I continued to seek help. I grew through levels of awareness as I continue to do today. Life always presents challenges. The difference is that today, I know that I can and will handle all that comes my way. I know this deep down in the recesses of my being. I will never judge anyone. I understand pain and I understand suffering. I understand that when someone is hurting, they are prone to do all manner of things. Those that do hurtful things, simply lack the tools to do otherwise. I also understand that there is a way home. Ways to find and give the tools. I, like you, am challenged by this daily. Finding new tools, growing and helping others to grow as well. I reach out my hand to you with this writing. It's up to you to take it.

Eden Wallace

FRANTIC

This Friday afternoon in 1979 was much like any
other. She would come home after school to an empty
house with her little brother in tow. Her mother and
father would not be there.

As she would enter the small brown duplex on 47th
Street, the panic would begin to nudge at her. She
would look at the tiny wooden clock with the little
yellow bird and the bird would scream "Hurry,
Hurry now!". She would go into the kitchen with the
orange, brown and yellow flowers making a dizzying
pattern on the tattered wallpaper, moving swiftly to
the orange rotator phone attached to the wall. Its cord
was long. So long that it tangled as she paced,
becoming more frantic. She would start dialing.
Listening and watching as each hole went around and
back again. There were three phone numbers she
would try, hoping that the mothers of the girls she
would call would say yes to her spending the
weekend. For the next two days she would be safe.
This Friday night, she would soon discover that
noone would be able to accommodate her request.

At nine years old she understood, by experience, that
if she did not find a safe place she would have to
endure one of two things; the inevitable screaming,
arguing, slapping and punching that would transpire
between her mother and father, or worse, much
worse, she would be delivered to the den of her

predator to be kept for the weekend where unspeakable things would happen.

This Friday, she did not find a haven. Her mother had called to say that she would not be going to Bingo that night, would be home soon, and to start supper. Normally, one would assume that this would bring relief to this girl, but she knew, at her tender age, that this was not good. She knew that her father was getting paid today. She knew this because of the "conversations" that she had tried not to overhear during the week.

Setting the orange receiver gently onto the cradle, she would make her way to her parents room. On this day nobody would know that she missed her mother. Missed her affection and protection so very much that she would step into their closet and wrap the arms of her mothers shirts and dresses around her. She would inhale as deeply as possible so she could smell her.

It seemed that her mother and father were never home. They both worked very hard to keep food on the table and the rent paid for the little brown duplex on 47th Street, however, they both worked equally hard at drinking and gambling that money away. There never seemed to be enough, and there most definitely was never any extra.

If you would ask the woman this little girl would later become, she would protect her mother and father and tell you that they did the best they could with what they had, but, if you asked the mother that this little girl would later become, she would not agree with that assumption. "Not even close.", she would say.

As she peeled potatoes she was thinking that the "Uncle" would not be an issue this weekend. Perhaps he would show up at one point, but she knew that as long as there was a witness nearby, she would not be pounced on like a tiny rabbit is snatched by a snarling, slobbering wolf. She was grateful that on this night, at least she would be safe from that. She resigned herself to what else would come that night.

When her mother arrived, they had dinner and she retreated to her barren little bedroom. A single bed, a dresser and again, wallpaper with a pattern that would stay in her mind forever. It was smattered with purple hippopotamuses and pink elephants, all smiling with googley eyes. During daylight she would smile back at them. At night she would fear those eyes...leering at her.

She picked up a book. She would read and count the minutes into hours until her father would come home. Not because she would then be able to see him, this man that she loved so much, but so she could be ready to move herself under her bed. She felt safest there. When the screaming, accusing and eventual sounds of fist hitting flesh would commence, she would trace the pattern of the reverse side of the Raggedy Ann & Andy bedspread, now thinned as it had covered her little bed ever since she could remember.

Some nights, when she anticipated taking to her hiding place, she would not have to. Her father would come home late into the night, long after her mother had retreated to her own bedroom. He would come in the door drunk and stumbling. The music would always come on, entirely too loud. He would eventually call out to the little girl. She knew what he wanted. He would want something to eat. Of course, he would have missed dinner and nothing would be left out for him, out of spite, she knew. He had replaced his family dinner with the liquid contents of any number of brown bottles.

The little girl would get up and go into the kitchen to make him something simple; eggs and toast. She would make this with love and care, knowing all the while that when she would bring it into the living room to him he would have already passed out. She never refused to get up and make him something. She knew she never could.

This particular Friday night in 1979 would be different and more memorable than any other night so far. This night her mother would come out into the living room and begin to poke at the viper. She would participate in the back and forth of name calling and insults. She would not give up the relentless prodding and poking, making sure that he felt her own venom seeping into his heart. Even at a mere nine years old, the little girl understood that her family was broken way beyond repair. She imagined it to be like a smashed porcelain doll, with limbs cracked and dangling and its face left in jagged pieces.

This night she would hear the pure anger in her father's voice and she knew it would be bad. She could almost taste the fear inside of her like the copper taste of blood.

This night it would escalate into a scene that not one child born onto this earth should ever have to witness. She was angry at her mother for provoking him. Didn't her mother know that soon he was going to come at her? The little girl would scream at them from under her bed to stop. STOP! Of course, they would not hear her and she would begin to wonder if she was screaming with her voice or only her mind.

When things started crashing and shattering she would want to run to get her little brother from his room at the end of the hall. She would dare not move though because she didn't want to SEE what was attached to what she could HEAR. She could only hope that her little brother would stay tucked safely away. She could hear him crying and begging for them to stop, just as she was. Hearing the desperation in her brother's voice filled her little body with rage.

On this night, at this moment, her father, flooded with his own rage, tipped over the olive green fridge with his bare hands. He then picked up one of the metal dining chairs and whipped it through the kitchen window. He would then corner his wife at the end of hall just outside of the door to the little girl's bedroom.

On this night, the little girl would come out of her hiding place from behind the thin veil of Raggedy Ann & Andy, because her mothers screams were more severe than any time before. She would walk out of her room to witness her father holding up a butcher knife to her mother's throat. He mother's face was red and swelling and her eyes were wide with terror. He father was spitting and snarling like a demon she only ever dreamed about.

It would be then that her tiny little instincts would kick in. She would grab her little brother and they would run, screaming, from the house and out into the cold moonlit street. She would keep running. They would run down the direct middle of the street looking for help from anyone who could hear them, knowing that the entire street must have heard everything, every time. Nobody would turn their porch light on of course, they never did.

Feeling frantic, they would reverse back down the street toward the place they had just escaped. What she hadn't realized was that her mother had gotten a call out to her aunt, to alert her that it was worse this time, much worse, and that she was afraid. The little girl would lead her little brother by his tiny little hand. She would notice that the echoing of screams had stopped. In her young mind she had no notion that the screams may have stopped due to her father slipping the blade of that butcher knife across the throat of her mother. She would be grateful for years after that this is not what had happened that night. She would come upon the house now lit with strobing blue and red lights, lighting up the yard in flashes as two police officers led her father away in hand cuffs towards the cruiser.

She would scream at them to not take her Daddy. She would scream that it was her mother's fault for not stopping. She didn't stop early enough, and she had pushed and pushed. The little girl was frantic and suddenly realized that she was wishing that the men in uniform would take both away. Take them away from her brother and herself. She was wishing that she never had to look at either one of them again.

It was on this night, that the hatred would start to seep into her tiny veins. She could feel it like a hot rush all over her body as she trembled with it. She now saw both of her parents as pathetic, from behind eyes tainted with ridicule and blame. Her father being dragged away with his feet tangling and stumbling over themselves, and her mother standing on the porch next to her sister, barely dressed in a ripped, almost transparent nightgown. They disgusted her. They were pathetic. She also realized in that moment, that time after time, she had been delivered into the hands of her predator so that they could get their addictions fed. Was it the addictions to the alcohol and gambling that were being met, or was it an addiction to chaos and pain. Did they only then feel alive?

It was on this night that she vowed to never be like her mother and to never let a man like her father enter her life. At the tiny age of nine years and seventeen days, she would become the most tragic thing that a young child can become. She would become a cynic. Quite certain that her life would be small and that she would never be given the chance at a life much beyond this one that she had been enduring. That little girl grew up that night. Her spirit withered and she knew that she did not have a chance.

Her father would come home. He always did, because her mother would never press charges against him. He would come home on another pay day and this time it would be the Christmas tree being savagely ripped apart to prove his drunken prowess. A few months ahead of that night, she would instinctively slip off her little jelly sandals and tip toe into the house through the back door to find her weeping mother in the arms of another man. She didn't understand then that her mother was seeking love and solace. She would begin to nurture a disdain and loathing for her mother, pity for her father and knowing that this nuclear family was a pathetic mess.

She would be horrified a year later to learn that her mother was pregnant with her sister. The sister she would protect with her life, but would never be able to grow close to due to circumstances and the dysfunction of her shattered family life.

The little girl would grow into a teen who would seek out the affection of any boy, just to feel noticed, loved.

She would become bitter and steeped in a sense of hopelessness. In her teen years, she would find herself living with her mother and her two siblings in a run down motel room in a run down town. Her father had gone to find work and had left them homeless. This was the final stage that was set for the last attack on her mother. This was the final time that her father would show up, put a knife to her mother's face and declare that he was going to end her. She would run out that night to the cop shop just down the street and alert the police herself. She hoped that this time they would again make it in time, and half hoping that this time the men in uniform would be too late. She was old enough now to take care of her brother and sister. If they were late, at least this time it would truly be over.

That teen would struggle for years to become a woman. With her mother and father finally separated for good, she would wander from place to place looking for her own safe haven, but instead finding addiction, abuse and rape. She would become a twenty something that would pull herself through college with the 'help' of an older male friend. She would struggle with addiction to block out the pain and the knowing that she did not truly belong any place. Through the grace of something unknown to her she made it past these years without overdosing or resorting to street life.

Today, this day, if you look at this woman, you might not be able to tell what horrors she has experienced, but for a little touch of sadness in her eyes when she smiles.

This woman has a family of her own now. She is a business woman, a passionate creative woman with a kind heart and a gentle soul. She can also summon the fierceness in her at the drop of a dime, should she feel threatened, abused or taken advantage of; one good thing, she would say, that she learned growing up. She got tough, wandering, looking for her place. Miraculously, she was able to keep a deep well of love flowing within her, if only on reserve.

This woman has made certain that she has broken every cycle of abuse, and now, even her addiction has left her in peace. She is clear minded and certain that she made it through those years so she could experience something grand, meant just for her.

She has chosen a man to be with and they have been resilient in rising from the flames of their own journey together. Their love has spanned more than two decades, and many more life times she suspects. She has chosen a gentle giant for protection. She has chosen a soulful warrior who, at the same time, will stop to meticulously release a dragon fly from a spider web, gently smiling as he watches it flutter away.

This woman, today, is madly and deeply in love with her brilliant 11 year old daughter. She looks at her some days, realizing that her daughter's experiences at 11 are so much more different than what had transpired for her. She takes great pride in that fact.

You would not know it, to look into the eyes of this woman, that there still exists that little nine-year-old girl, so frantic for her family to be 'normal'. She has no relationship with her own mother, sister or brother, and is only now, 35 years later, beginning to live in a place of forgiveness for her father.

You wouldn't know that too many nights within the depths of her dreams she returns to that little brown duplex on 47th Street to relive the moments with the orange phone, never quite able to recall the number she is trying to dial for salvation. She wakes often in the middle of the night to the echo of her own screams.

Through some form of grace, that little girl, abused, tattered and torn, has grown out of violence and hopelessness into a woman desperate to help heal the world, and in that service, to secure the ultimate healing place for herself. That little girl and this woman will always be one. The only difference between the two being the girl feared the experiences of her young life, the woman fears not using those experiences to help others. She lives her life for that little girl who resides within her and for the little girl that has come from inside of her.

Cycles are broken and the future holds beauty and wonder. The kind of awe that a child has when she realizes the world is in the palm of her hand.

Love for the First Time
by Lisa James

It was the summer I left the eighth grade. The
summer that, afterwards, I would enter into my
freshman year and officially become a high schooler.
The summer my dating life would take a turn in a
new direction and I would experience love for the
first time. It was the summer I was scorched by
Cupid's Arrow.

I was introduced to my first boyfriend through my
best friend. My best friend was dating his best friend,
and somehow, like best friends do, a blind date was
discussed. The blind date was arranged, and before I
knew it, I was meeting the boy for the first time. We
met at my house for an informal evening of movies
and popcorn (and parental authority within ear shot).
I was in instant awe of this specimen in front of me.
He was tall, with dark hair and these dark brown eyes
that penetrated my soul with their gaze. He held my
attention, and almost immediately, my heart. He was
older than I, a rising senior. What luck to have an
older man interested in me! To be a freshman dating a
senior was instant status, proven by the class ring that
accompanied my finger, regardless of the social circle
in which you hovered. The ring was not the round,
familiar design that was popular among the buyers of
memories trying so desperately to secure four years
of their lives into one piece of tangible metal and
semi-precious gem, but it was instead, rectangular in
design with a raised "HH" on the stone. The design
was reflective of the design of his body, long and

lean. Every girl dreamed of wearing a class ring, and I was finally one of the lucky ones. To wear a class ring was symbolic. The ring showed the world I was no longer alone, that I was now dating, and that someone out there was interested in me.

I was wearing my boyfriend's ring on the day of orientation for my freshman year. I went to a small Christian school, so I know the news of my "being taken" would spread quickly. I was not known for having boyfriends. I hadn't even experienced my first real kiss or post-relationship heartbreak yet. And I hadn't even gone on a real date. But the news spread. Soon, people started to hear I was dating someone, someone from the public high school, someone who was a senior.

The one guy I who I was interested in dating for quite some time but who never conveyed the same interest in me... he was the sole person at school I needed to hear the news. The news finally reached him. He walked straight up to me in the gymnasium on that orientation day, picked up my hand, looked at the ring, then turned around and walked away. This guy, who was my first real crush, began to show interest in me after I started dating. I guess he figured if I was good enough for a senior from the town's public high school, then maybe he had been mistaken about me. Maybe there was something there he had overlooked. But he never got the chance to find out. This guy left me feeling rejected and unworthy of love, which may be the reason for the instant awe and the hasty decision to begin a relationship with my boyfriend.

Rebounding from my crush set up a destiny of failures in dating from that point on.

My boyfriend and I, we were not a typical couple. I was fourteen and he was almost eighteen. I was not allowed to go on dates at that age, and, if by some miracle, I was allowed to go out, I had an early curfew. Staying out until midnight on a Friday or Saturday night was out of the question. When we went on a date, which was very rare, I was always escorted by my mom. One time, he wanted to take me to get something to eat from Subway. My mom drove us there, we went in (my mom stayed in the car) and I ordered my usual: the Subway Cold Cut Trio. We didn't stay to eat; instead we took the food back to my house. He never minded coming to the house to spend time with me, which at this point was practically every day. We spent our time in the game room at the back of the house, listening to music and playing Nintendo, or watching TV or movies. We loved to dance to our song, or see who could out-do whom in Zelda.

The only time my mom made an exception to my curfew was for a special occasion like a Christmas party or an invite to the prom. Since I was dating a senior, it was implied I would, as a matter of fact, attend his senior prom. Although the prom was months away, I knew I would be going with him. I planned months in advance on what I would wear, how I would fix my hair, the shoes that would match the perfect dress, and even what I would eat when we went to dinner beforehand. To go to the prom was like a fairy tale come to life. The fantasy and beauty and alternate reality were part of that teenage utopia I was going to get to experience and I was so excited!

On one of those special occasions in which I was allowed to stay out past curfew, my boyfriend and I went to a Christmas party/dance for a girl's organization in which I was a member. I was nervous about taking my boyfriend to the party. The organization, The Rainbow Girls, is a Christian-based organization associated with the Free Masons. I was scared "they" wouldn't approve of my boyfriend. Also, I wasn't much of a dancer, and we hadn't really been on many dates, so the whole experience was new for me. The party was decorated with Christmas lights and a tree, and the food was prepared in the finger-food fashion typical of a teenage dance. We had meatballs and Lil' Smokies, ham and pimento cheese sandwiches, and this amazing 7UP punch. There was a DJ for entertainment, and the center of the room was for dancing. The guests lined the floor most of the night, with a few brave stragglers making it to the dance floor every-once-in-a-while to dance to one of their favorite songs. My boyfriend and I danced a few times to slower songs, and of course to "our song." It was definitely a night to remember.

It was also the last party we would attend together, the closest I would be to attending his prom. A few weeks before the prom, I received a phone call. I answered the phone in anticipation of hearing his voice, yet the tone of the caller was enough to make my stomach turn.

"Lisa, I have something to tell you," said a sad, familiar voice.

"What is it?" I asked. I was unsure I even wanted to hear the answer to the question I was sure was rhetorical.

"I want to make this short, so I will just tell you," he said. "I think we don't need to see each other anymore."

I was in shock before the final word fell out of his mouth. "What did he just say?" I questioned to myself. Did I just hear that correctly?

"What do you mean we shouldn't see each other anymore?" I managed to mutter while choking back tears.

"I just think it's for the best," was all he could reply.

"Please don't do this," I managed to plea through a now tear-stained voice. "Please don't break up with me. I love you."

"I love you, too, but this is what I feel is best. I am so sorry to do this, but I have to go. Goodbye."

And he hung up.

In one phone call, he managed to take away everything that was my teenage world and the anticipation of what walking in my world would be, but more than that, he shattered my dreams of going to the prom with the boy I loved. I obviously wouldn't be attending the highlight of his senior year with him, and it was already too late. Prom was right around the corner. Plans for going to the prom have to be made well in advance, and I only had a couple of weeks. Instead of participating in one of my teenage rites, I sat home that fanciful evening and wondered: wondered who his date was, wondered what she looked like, wondered how her shoes looked with her hair and dress, wondered if she was prettier than me, wondered what he looked like in that tuxedo. I pondered how the decorations looked, how the food smelled, how the punch tasted and if someone had actually spiked it, and how the band sounded. I panicked when I thought he might actually dance with *her* to *our* song. I cried myself to sleep, envisioning a world of beauty and euphoria, even if only temporary. A world I did not have the pleasure or invitation to join.

After the prom, I received another phone call from my now ex-boyfriend, this time asking me to forgive him and start dating him again. Once again, I submitted to his request. As it turns out, this would be the last and final time I would take him back. The relationship ended, but the destructive path that was our relationship formed the foundation for many toxic relationships to come.

My first boyfriend and I dated for nine months. During those nine months, we broke up five times. Each breakup was more emotionally damaging than the first. Each excuse was crazier than the previous. Each make-up filled with more disbelief than the last. I was new to romantic love and relationships with boys. I was young and vulnerable and inexperienced. I didn't know any better. I didn't know I shouldn't have allowed the unmanned elevator ride to continue. I didn't know when I stepped out of it and shut the doors the first time that I should have kept them closed. We did love each other, although the love I felt then was immature and new. The pattern that entwined our relationship was a pattern that followed me for the majority of my life the summer I was scorched by Cupid's arrow.

Fast forward twenty three years, and here I am, telling you the beginning of my story of cyclical abuse and toxic relationships. I always dreamed of living life large, but I allowed doubt to hold me back. The doubt stemmed from a series of terrible romantic relationships. I chose the wrong guy so many times over. I chose the guy without a stable childhood, or who hated his dad and despised his mom. I chose those men who held onto the pain of their past and used it to fuel their anger and pain during their present. I allowed men into my life that treated me like garbage or told me I wouldn't find anyone else to love me. I allowed those men to shout poison darts into my mind and soul. Years of mental and emotional abuse had me believing that I was never good enough, even though everything I was doing with my life proved otherwise. I was a perfect housewife and mother, or I was in college, or I graduated with a chemistry degree, or I was working in pharmaceutical research, or I had an amazing career in the Army, or, or, or…

I lived my life in a whirlwind of vengeance. I wanted to prove to these men I was worth more than their small, narrow minds thought of me. This mode of thinking actually caused me to pursue achievements I, under normal circumstances, would have never thought I could accomplish. But I wasn't living my life for me. I wasn't pursuing my passions and my dreams. I was living my life to prove these men wrong. I was living for revenge. Yet, while I was ultimately successful, the doubt was still there, hiding in the recesses of my mind, a festering boil that poisoned my spirit.

Fast forward to now. I am in a great relationship with an amazing man. He is supportive and encouraging despite my setbacks along the journey to figuring out who I am and what I want to do with my life both personally and professionally. The journey to figuring out who I am and what I want (after so many years of being who I was shaped from the abuse and toxicity) has been bumpy and curvy and straight and narrow and wide and sometimes even upside down, but it has been a remarkable journey nonetheless. And I'm grateful for the interesting ride.

Although born to parents who have been married for 50 years to the same person, Lisa James' romantic history is full of toxic and devastating relationships. Her past is filled with mental and emotional abuse, cheating partners, unwanted sexual encounters, fights, anger, desperation, self-loathing, loss of self, and a ton of self-doubt. She repeated toxic romantic relationship patterns under the facade of the "God Complex" and the belief that she could help a person change their life for the better. Every once in a while, a good man would enter her life and show her how a romantic relationship was supposed to work, yet she would push them away because she didn't know or feel her self-worth. The cyclical pattern of toxic relationships continued viciously, with some being worse than others. It wasn't until 2008 when her journey started to change ever-so-slightly from a history of toxic relationships to one full of love and trust. She now lives every day in a positive relationship free of toxicity and full of love and support. Oh, and she is definitely resilient.

Lisa James currently resides in a suburb of San Antonio, TX, with her children and fiancé, as well as their five snakes, four dogs, three cats, one prairie dog, and one tortoise. No, they currently do not own a partridge in a pear tree.

You can find Lisa here:
Blogtalk Radio: Rabbit Hole Reflections with Lisa James
Transform Your Life with Kellie and Lisa
Facebook: facebook.com/lisa.vanslyke1
Twitter: @wanderwithlisaj
Email: wanderwithlisaj@gmail.com

**"You know I didn't mean it.
Why'd you make me do that to you?"**

One woman's story of emotional and physical abuse, death and resurrection.

(quiet crying in the background) Miss Elsner. Miss Elsner.
Blackness
Silence
Quiet

Sitting up violently I pull the tube out of my mouth it seems to be ten feet long I am choking, where am I and why is this tube in my mouth, why are these people looking at me crazy?

"She's back, she's back," says one of the guys in a white coat. "Miss Elsner, are you okay can you hear me?"

Of course I can hear the guy he is pretty much yelling at me in a small area.

What the hell happened? I remember, I went to see my ex the abuser he wanted to talk it starts to come back to me...yelling...   him throwing me against the wall telling me we have to get back together because he fucking loves me... my lips bleeding....my head hurts...

"Miss Elsner you've been unconscious for some time we thought we had lost you, do you remember what happened, do you know what year it is?"

What is up with all the questions, I am trying to piece back together how I got here, why didn't I fight, he was kneeling on my shoulders with his hands around my throat, I remember I could not breathe, a cracking sound, the pressure in my chest

Blackness

Quiet

"Miss Elsner, do you know what year it is?"

I look at the Doctor for the first time, really stop and take a ragged breath and look at him and slowly I say, quietly… it's 2004, who found me and did the police get him…

"Am I safe?"

The last word hangs in the air and the Doctor smiles, "Yes, Miss Elsner, you are safe, and he is in custody. Now lay back down. You need to rest."

It floods me, reality. I went to talk to him after three months of no contact. *Why?* The bruises from the last beating were healed. My mind was starting to heal. I was starting to love myself and learn who I am; who I am without the verbal abuse telling me I am stupid, fat, dumb… all the names he said. The amount of emotional wear and tear on me was profound. I was not the outgoing, positive girl I was meant to be. Our relationship was centered around cocaine use, going to little bars around town during the week and larger house parties and raves on weekends. I do not think we were ever sober together. I do not believe that justifies the abuse, but it did not help to stop it or give me clarity to see how bad of a situation I was in.

I lived with that man for eleven months after six months of dating. He never hit me while we dated. It started the third week we lived together. I remember it so well - it was a Wednesday night. We had dinner and sex in the living room and I stood up to get a drink. When I turned around and started to walk back to the couch, he was up and met me in the kitchen, grabbed me and asked me what the hell I thought I was doing? I was confused. I said, "getting a drink and coming back to you," he said, "fuck that I didn't say you could get up or come back" and bam he put his fist into my cheek and I fell backwards the glass in my hand shattered I cut myself trying to stand back up, naked. Tears streaming down my face I didn't know what to feel or think, and he just stood there darkness in human form not saying a word but looking at me as if I was pathetic, and I felt such fear and rage and confusion. "What the hell is wrong with you," I said. He crossed the distance between us and said, "Oh babe I'm sorry you know I didn't mean it."

That was the first time but not the last.

We are at my family cabin in the north woods of Wisconsin on a four-wheeler ride. We stop for a break to make out under a tree. I lay my head on his, lap he strokes my hair. Hard. He starts to bring me to my feet and hit me on top of the head and proceeds to hit my ribs with his fist asking me if I brought him here to tell my dad what he does to me and to keep my mouth shut. I once again was baffled. We were being close, intimate. Why did he do this? I cry. He says don't cry mary why do you make me do these things to you, it's gonna be all right you just have to know I love you and you don't need to tell your dad that I fuck up sometimes, okay?

Baffled. Shocked. Scared. Embarrassed. Enraged.

I felt so alone that weekend visiting with dad, allowing him to get to know my new boyfriend, thinking I should say something to him for help but would he believe me? Would he kill the guy? What would happen? I said nothing. I did nothing to protect myself from another threatening situation. I did not love or respect myself enough to ask for help or tell someone what was happening to me on a weekly basis.

After months of beatings that only got worse, I finally told a coworker. She rallied a team of four women to move me out and get me to a safe place and we did it in a few hours, I think. Me and my cat were out and I was ok. Within three days, I was moved out of our apartment and free from the abuse. He tried to stop by my work, but the girls always had my back and kept him away. Why I went back that fateful night escapes me today, but I almost lost my life because of it.

Today I am in love with a man who supports me, loves me, makes real love to me and knows who I am. He knows my insecurities I have in my mind and with my body and he takes the time to break down the barriers to introduce me to pleasure and teach me about love and all that goes with it emotionally and carnally. I am no longer a victim. Even though I still have old behaviors that were caused by that relationship of abuse, I learned who I am without the abuse. I always ate my eggs scrambled because that is how my abuser ate his when in all actuality, I like mine over medium so I can dip my toast in them. Today, I eat my eggs the way I like. Today I love myself. I recommend all women purchase *Simple Abundance by Saran Ann Breathnach.* THIS book saved me and taught me to live an authentic and simple life loving myself. She has daily readings to learn to love again, and I realize it has to start with me.

As the years went by and I was removed from the abuse, I got better. I received a call four years later and was informed that he was being released from jail and there would be a five-year restraining order in place. I didn't care. He was gone from me forever. I had to block him and his family on Facebook because they all tried to find me, but that is over and done. As I write this, I realize it's been over ten years, and I can still remember the horrible way he made me feel. Today, I know I never have to feel that way again.

What many women in an abusive relationship fail to realize is it NEVER stops or gets better. It cannot. It will not. As soon as a mean word is said, a punch is thrown, or the slow tearing down of your character with snide comments and jokes starts, that is your cue from the universe to leave. Leave, call for help, get help, and get out. The pain will end. You will realize your worth and that he is incapable of loving you because he does not love himself.

Mary Kay Elsner is an eclectic, recovered, eccentric, positive force to be reckoned with. As an avid reader and lover of words, she has been an MC for over 20 years. Her music, recorded, written and performed under the spirit and name of Spryte © has been heard on stages throughout the Midwest and across the United States since 1992. Mary Kay writes about her past in third person and it is not where she is any longer.

"I love the opportunity to share my story and heal from it each time. I am so blessed today to worship the Creator I strive to please and the magic in my life by the women I choose to call friends and sisters. We all have a story to share and it's a lovely message to the women who come after us that we truly are better in numbers. My spirit today soars when I share the wreckage of my past and the beauty of what my life is today."

My music, my ministry, my Master's degree, my mind, and my emotions are at your service.

Blessings in love and light,

Mary Kay Elsner Spryte ©
Masters Penn State
B.S. Psychology
A.A.S. Anthropology

Find me on Facebook in Spiritual Seeds Sown by Spryte ©

Final thoughts from Kellie Fitzgerald.

Anyone who has listened to one of my shows, or read something I've written or attended an event or workshop I've been involved with already knows my story. The reason I jumped at the chance to compile this book with Lisa was not to tell my story again but to show there are so many similar stories and each and every one of those stories needs to be told.

See, when we share our own stories we not only heal ourselves, but we give others the chance to heal right along with us. When I was going through my incredibly abusive first marriage I truly believed I was the only person ever to have such a story. I thought that even if I did reach out and tell someone what I was going through they wouldn't believe me - or they would think it was all my own fault.

Even when I'd put that whole experience behind me and moved on with my life I still held on to bits and pieces of that abuse. I still struggled to find learn who I really was. I still had a tendency to jump out of my skin whenever anyone even tried to hug me. Battle scars. I had oh so many battle scars.

It really wasn't until I started writing about my story, and telling my story, and owning my story that I began to discover myself...and started to really heal from my experiences. Really, this happened accidentally when I was asked to teach a journaling workshop at a battered women's shelter. I saw how one person sharing something that had happened to them encouraged others to share their own stories. That day in that workshop I witnessed how beautifully broken people can be and how truly splendid it is when they discover their own light pouring through those broken pieces. One by one, like phoenixes rising from the ashes, each woman found strength in the sharing of her own personal story not only through journaling but through actively telling her own story and passionately and lovingly listening to the stories of others. Truly this was a workshop where I became not an instructor but a very willing participant in a life-altering event.

Of course it is not only women who are battered. During my travels I have met many very brave men who have come forward and shared their own stories of abuse. I've learned that children who have witnessed the abuse of a parent or sibling are as traumatized as those who are actively beaten. I've learned everyone has a different way of coping with their abuse history and that often those coping mechanisms are not healthy. I've learned that while we've come a very long way as a society there is still a very long way to go before domestic violence is a thing of the past.

In reading the stories in this book I hope you've learned some things too. It is my hope you've learned about the resilience of the human spirit, how very sad beginnings can have very happy endings and perhaps most of all I hope you've learned domestic violence really impacts people from every conceivable walk of life, age, sex, religion etc. Domestic violence is not a problem of the poor, or of the uneducated or even of one race or part of the world or country. I would guess every one of us knows someone who has either been abused in the past or is being abused right now whether we know it or not. It's time to have honest open discussions about domestic violence. It's time to stop trying to sweep it under the rug or whisper rumors in hushed tones. It's time to shout from the rooftops how it is never OK to abuse anyone else. It's time to say "enough" of people hurting other people.

It's time to teach our children how to stand up for themselves but more importantly than standing up for themselves it's time to teach our children how to be kind; how to accept everyone else's beliefs no matter how different from our own. We need to teach our children compassion, self-esteem and love of self and others.

If you or someone you know is being abused, no matter what type of abuse it is, please reach out and seek help. Know that you are important, your life matters, and there is most definitely a bright, happy and successful life after abuse...I know, I've been there.

If you want more information about my particular story or how you can help end domestic violence feel free to email kellie@ibbilanepress.com. Thanks so much for reading the stories in this book, feel free to share it everyone!